DID YOUR G
COME IVI
THE COUNTY MAYO?

Anne Marie Ryan

ARTHUR H. STOCKWELL LTD.
Elms Court   Ilfracombe
Devon

ISBN 0 7223 2193-7
Printed in Great Britain by
Arthur H. Stockwell Ltd.
Elms Court   Ilfracombe
Devon

Contents

The Duck Pond

When I was a child I spent quite a lot of time with my grandmother one way and another. It usually came about because my family had been on holiday and had returned to Glasgow, where we lived, leaving me behind as company for Gran. Gran was always a great one for a bit of company. The periods varied from a few weeks to a few months, depending on when my Aunt Mary could accompany me back. What that did to my general education can be imagined, but as my father was in the army a certain amount of moving about was to be expected anyway, and in those days it was not considered so important for a girl to be educated, she was usually expected to marry.

During the longer stays I attended the village school. I liked that. I was very much more advanced than the country children and was often allowed to assist my teacher with the younger ones or, perhaps, a particularly backward child with reading or writing problems. On looking back now I can see and appreciate that Mrs Kennedy took quite a lot of trouble with me. I was excused Irish, which was obligatory for everyone else, because it would not be of any use to me, and instead was set special lessons in English, geography and arithmetic which she worked out for me alone so I should be better equipped for when I returned to Scotland.

"Can't have you letting us down too much now, can we?" she would say with a smile.

The school consisted of two rooms, one for the infants, and the larger one for girls up to fourteen years of age, the then leaving age, and the boys had similar accommodation. Although Mrs Kennedy sometimes got really exasperated with her charges, which was understandable as it was not easy either for her or for us with such differing ages and standards all in the same room, she was essentially a very kind person and really had our best interests at heart. The best days, to my mind at least, were when the weather was very wet or wintry, as then quite a few of the pupils who lived a long way from the school would be absent. No such thing as cars or buses in those days, you walked everywhere you wanted to go, or if you were lucky, you might have a battered old bike.

On these especially cold and wintry days Mrs Kennedy had an arrangement with one of her pupils, who lived near the school, to light the fire, which was the only form of heating, about an hour before opening time so the room would be nice and warm for us, and would provide a hot drink of tea for the poor, wet, bedraggled children who had trudged, some for miles, through the weather to attend class.

On these days our usual lessons would be curtailed and we would gather round the fire and read aloud to one another, lovely stories of fairies, goblins, leprechauns, the giant Finn MacCool. The favourite ones of all were *Aesop's Fables*, and I can see now, as clearly as if it was yesterday, the looks of utter absorption, mixed with horror, at the tale of the murderer, standing on the steps of the gallows and biting off the ear of his own mother blaming her for his predicament because of her lack of chastisement in his youth.

At Christmas, Mrs Kennedy would give every child a little gift, a small beaded purse, or an embroidered handkerchief, a fancy slide or comb, beads, and a few sweets, and the pleasure this gave was out of all proportion to the value of the gifts. Some of the children were very poor indeed and presents were very few and far between I can tell you.

For me there was always a book, *Great Expectations, Little Women* and my favourite *Another Day* by Jeffery Farnol. I treasured it then, I treasure it still.

I used to do little chores for Gran such as getting a few things from the village shop, or perhaps a small can of fresh water from the village pump; but my main one was to go for the milk each evening; and on this particular evening Gran handed me the little can kept for the purpose and I set off to walk the half mile or so to the farm.

As I drew near I looked anxiously to see if Kathleen, my best friend, was anywhere to be seen. She waited for me whenever she could and I was always delighted to see her, as she would affectionately link arms and escort me across the farmyard to the dairy where, if I was lucky, the milking would be finished and I could get my can filled and escape. My heart sank, there was no sign of Kathleen. I would have to brave whatever particular torture was in store for me, alone. That yard held countless terrors for me. I never knew what I'd meet there. It could be bullocks; cows; goats; pigs; ganders; turkey cocks; dogs, several, of all shapes and sizes, and all barking furiously at me; or last, but by no means least; the Rileys themselves.

There were a lot of them. There was the eldest girl, a big strong comely lass who would be about sixteen at this time, rejoicing in the nickname of Doodle, and her father's right hand. He always maintained that she was worth two of any of the lads when it came to doing the work of the farm. My most abiding memory of Doodle is of haymaking time; those long warm wonderful days, with every kid in the village hitching a ride on the bogies, a sort of long wooden platform on wheels which was pushed under the haycock to transport it to the farm, and Doodle, with her laughing freckled face, blue eyes dancing and brown hair flying as she handled the horses with every bit as much skill as any of the men.

A few days previously we had watched as the men had cut the meadow, swinging the scythes in wide arcs, effortlessly hour after hour, every precious good day was vital if the hay was to be dried and gathered into the barn. Those were the days when the harsh cry of the corncrake was often heard; alas no more, modern machinery had seen to that. Occasionally we found a nest with eggs in it, and once a little clutch of chicks, huddling terrified in the long grass, and a little patch was left round them for protection until their mother should return to them. The corncake ranked second only to the cuckoo, the announcer that spring had come, in the affections of the country folk.

Sometimes we helped a little in the turning and gathering of the hay, but mostly we just lay on our backs revelling in the sun and the scent of the sweet new-mown hay listening to the song of the skylark and marvelling how that tiny fluttering speck could produce such a loud joyful sound. Or we would play, chasing one another from one end of the field to the other, playing hide and seek amongst the haycocks, until the day that Kathleen jumped down from the middle of a cock where she had been hiding right on to the prongs of a pitchfork which had been carelessly left and was hidden by loose hay, and one of the prongs went right through her foot. She was rushed to hospital and emerged a few weeks later seemingly none the worse for the experience; but it had a very sobering effect and after that Gran would not let me play in the fields again.

After Doodle, came two brawny lads, Pat and Mick; then Nuala, a younger edition of Doodle, who mostly helped her mother in the kitchen; then Gerry; then Kathleen, who was different from the other two girls being thin with black hair and brown eyes; and several more younger ones; and I, a skinny nervous townie from Glasgow was fair game for them all. There was not an ounce of malice amongst the lot of them, just plain rough and tumble high spirits.

Kathleen could usually be relied on to provide some protection from their teasing but she was not above joining in the fun herself, such as hopping off the see-saw whilst I was in mid-air, or enticing me to the haybarn by promising to show me the newest kittens, pups or chicks, where the lads would be lying in wait ready to pounce. On one occasion having lured me to the haybarn loft on the pretext of giving me some apples to take home to Gran, she darted out, slamming the trapdoor behind her, leaving me in darkness amidst the spiders and other creepy-crawlies, petrified and half fainting with panic, and the suffocating, sweet smell of the apples. And there they left me, occasionally emitting hollow groans and mournful howls, amidst gusts of stifled laughter, for what seemed an age.

I looked through the gate cautiously and was relieved to see that there were only a few hens and an odd duck or two about, so I opened it and hurried across the yard to the dairy. I was almost there when suddenly Pat and Mick, my chief tormentors, burst out of the haybarn, white goose feathers stuck in their curly mops, and whooping wildly bore down on me. I dropped the can and turned to flee but they soon caught me and each taking an arm they pulled me outside the gates and over to the duck pond and holding me suspended over the water shouted "One, two, three and in she goes" pulling me back just as my nose was about to go in.

"Now then" shouted Pat to Mick "this time we'll get it right. Both together now — One, two, three" repeating the same maneouvre of pulling me back just in time.

I had always hated that duck pond. It was full of black peaty water, gloomy looking with its overhanging trees, the edges filthy with thick green scum and goose and duck droppings.

At that moment Kathleen appeared and came flying to my aid, with disastrous results, as Mick, in endeavouring to beat off her furious assault, loosed his hold on my arm, and I slithered in sideways getting well coated almost up to the waist. Luckily Pat still retained his grip on the other arm and quickly pulled me out, and I just stood there oozing slime. The three of them gazed at me aghast for a few moments but soon they started to laugh helplessly even while they tried to clean me up a bit with tufts of grass. Useless of course, so I set off home, squelching and dripping, leaving them rolling about on the grass hysterical with mirth.

When I got home I called to Gran through the half-door and when she saw the state of me she cried out in horror.

"God bless us, child, what in the world happened to ye?"

"I fell in the duck pond" I wailed.

"Hush now, agradh, hush" she said soothingly as she got out papers and made me stand on them whilst she emptied hot water from the large kettle, which was always kept ready on the range, into the old tin bath.

She called Aunt Mary and Uncle Ned to come and have a look at me.

"What happened to her?" asked Aunt Mary.

"She says she fell in the duck pond" said Gran.

"Fell me eye" snorted Aunt Mary. "Pushed more like."

"Yes" said Uncle Ned "that would be more like. That lot are as wild as a bunch of mountain goats!"

"An' she didn't bring anny milk for the sup o' tay ayther" said Gran "so ye better go down and get it Ned."

"I will that" said Uncle Ned and he got on his bike with a glint in his eye that boded ill for the Rileys, large and small, when he caught up with them.

Gran stripped all the clothes off me, put me in the bath and scrubbed me vigorously to remove every trace of the horrible muck.

"That lot are for burning annyway" said Aunt Mary eyeing the filthy pile of clothes balefully.

"Ah well" said Gran philosophically "I suppose we must be grateful she didn't swaller a couple av mouthfuls as well."

Soon Uncle Ned came back with the milk and handing it to Gran said "I'll go for it from now on. A right den av lions that place is and Jen's no Daniel to be thrown to thim each evenin', are ye now?" he teased as he put his arm around my shoulders and gave me an affectionate hug.

Minding Jack

One particularly fine morning during our holidays, my mother had announced her intention of cycling into the nearest small township — a matter of about five miles — to do some shopping. She accordingly set out, bright and early, leaving me and my little brother Jack, in the care of Gran and Aunt Mary.

I was about seven years old at this time, and Jack was almost four. He was a great favourite with everyone; he was such a happy little lad, with dancing blue eyes and fair hair, and, though I loved him as much as anyone, I must confess that sometimes I felt a little bit put out at the amount of attention he received, and would usually wander off disconsolately to pay my good friends, the Behan brothers, a visit at their little forge at the end of the village. I spent hours in that fascinating place, watching Paddy and Mick as they hammered and turned, hammered and turned, as the red-hot metal gradually took shape, sparks flying and anvil ringing, and both of them black as the ace of spades in their long leather aprons.

I liked most of all to watch when there was a horse to be shod. Where we lived was racehorse country, and a fine sight indeed it was to see the strings of thoroughbreds exercising first thing every morning, but Paddy and Mick never had one of those aristocrats in their forge, at least I never saw one, they dealt with the quiet patient old farm horses standing motionless, head down, just looking tired.

I said as much to Paddy once. "Ah, shure an' he's only havin' forty winks for himself" he said.

I looked at his twinkling eyes suspiciously.

"True, darlin' true! Don't ye know that horses can sleep standin' up?" he said laughing as he swung me up on its back for a little jaunt back to the farm.

As we were sitting having our breakfast Gran came into the kitchen with the basket which she used to collect the eggs on her arm.

"Bad scran to those ole hins annyway" she said showing the bare half dozen eggs in the basket. "They're all goin' broody, must be layin' out somewhere. You and me Jen'll have a look later on to see if we can find a nest or two in the hedges."

She pulled the large earthenware crock in which she kept her eggs out from the larder and carefully added the half dozen to the few already in the crock.

"Give us a couple av thim eggs for the cake" said Aunt Mary, who was mixing a large currant soda cake in a bowl at the kitchen table.

"Arrah, I have nary a one to spare, as ye well know" said Gran, turning again to count the eggs in the crock.

At that precise moment Jack jumped down from his chair, ran over to Gran where she crouched on her hunkers on the floor, and threw his arms round her neck in a hearty hug with the result that they both overbalanced and down he sat full square in the crock on the precious eggs.

Gran pulled him off quickly and sat ruefully surveying the damage. Aunt Mary came to have a look also.

"There, now" she said "ye had a right to give us an egg whin I asked ye," adding rather gleefully "I'll have enough now annyway."

Gran said nothing just salvaged the two or three still intact and then handing the rest to Aunt Mary to do what she would with them.

"Here, Jen" said Aunt Mary "take Jack out to play for a bit from under our feet. We're fallin' over wan another in here. Mind him well though!"

I did so reluctantly. Looking after Jack was a full-time job, and once outside, as usual, he made a bee-line for the village pump. He took great delight in splashing about in the concrete bowl which surrounded the pump and took the overflow, and, after a little while, I left him there playing quite happily whilst I wandered off in search of a few cowslips or other wild flowers to take home to Gran for her little altar.

Suddenly I heard Jack screaming in terror, and when I looked round I saw with horror that Mrs Magillicuddy's flock of geese, led by a particularly vicious old gander, had Jack surrounded. Having had several close encounters with that old gander myself in the past, all of which he had won hands down, he only had to raise his head and cock a wicked eye in my direction to cause me to give him a very wide berth indeed; so I well knew the hazards of approaching him; but I had to do it, so I flew into the honking, hissing melee, scooped up Jack and took off as fast as I could, and that was pretty fast I can tell you. There can be few things more calculated to lend wings to your heels than a furious hissing gander, neck outstretched to nip, pounding along in your rear. It took Gran and old Mrs Magillicuddy, both armed with yard brushes, several minutes to beat him off; but neither of us was much the worse, I collected a couple of painful little nicks, but he had not been able to get a really good beakful of my leg.

Poor old Mrs Magillicuddy was very apologetic, but I did not tarry long in her company for, truth to tell, I was more afraid of her than of the gander. She looked just as I imagined the witches in the fairy tales I was always reading would look, so thin that she was hardly more than skin and bone, sparse, straggly white hair scraped up in a tight knot, and her face had that dark peat-brown look that came from continually standing over the smoky open fire in the tumbledown cottage she occupied a little apart from the main cluster of houses in the village; but, most of all, she had a large disfiguring goitre, a common affliction in those parts at the time. She had been a widow for many years, had no family, and, somehow or other kept body and soul together by selling the milk from her few goats, eggs, chickens, and her geese at Christmas.

She appeared at the half-door to the kitchen soon afterwards with a small peace offering of a few eggs, which, after the mishap of the morning, Gran was very pleased to accept; and in return, Gran cut a large wedge from the currant

soda cake which Aunt Mary had just taken out of the oven, added a pot of home-made gooseberry jam, and she went off delighted.
   "Poor, harmless, unfort'nate auld craytur she is" said Gran sympathetically.

In the afternoon, Gran and I set off to search the hedgerows in the meadow at the back of the cottages to see if we could find a nest. We searched for some time without success and were on the point of giving up when Gran caught hold of my arm.
   "Whist now, agradh" she said "it's that little brown speckly wan, just as I thought. We'll watch to see where she goes," and looking where she pointed I saw the little hen making her way speedily and very purposefully towards the corner of the meadow. We followed and sure enough there she was sitting on a nest very cleverly concealed in a little thicket of gorse. She rose with a squawk as Gran made a grab to catch her and we saw several eggs in the nest.
   Gran gathered them up and put them in her apron.
   "What are you going to do with them, Gran?" I asked.
   "Well, agradh" said Gran "as she's so determined to be a mother I think we'll let her hatch out a clutch av chicks, but in my hinhouse where I can look after thim."
   We made our way home with the little speckled hen running very agitatedly in our wake, but after Gran had arranged the eggs in a nesting box she happily settled down on them, and I could look forward also to the day when the little chicks made their appearance.

When we went into the kitchen my mother had arrived back from her shopping trip with a little gift for both Jack and me, a furry bunny with a squeak for him and a book of fairy tales for me. We sat down to new-laid eggs, home-made wheaten and currant soda bread with some of Gran's gooseberry jam, to which we all did full justice; and afterwards I opened my book and I did not take my nose out of it until it was time for bed.
   In the meantime Jack was having a great time with his bunny, running up to everyone in turn and squeaking energetically in their ear, until, at last Gran said "Time for bed,

Jack, you too Jen."

When we were washed and dressed in our night clothes, Gran sat in the old rocking-chair, with Jack on her lap and me beside her to say the prayers together.

"God Bless Mummy, God Bless Daddy" she commenced and as she went through the list she became aware of Jack casting anxious glances at Uncle Ned where he sat with head bowed at the kitchen table listening. Wondering what he would do she carried on, still omitting Uncle Ned, and was fast running out of names when Jack could stand it no longer and jumped up shouting "And what about God Bless Uncle Ned over there!" looking very accusingly at Gran. "Oh, all right then" said Gran. "God Bless Uncle Ned over there." Jack repeated it very emphatically after her and then went over to give Uncle Ned an especially affectionate hug and goodnight kiss with a very noticeably cooler one for Gran, before trotting off to bed with his beloved old battered teddy under one arm and his new plaything, the bunny, under the other.

The next morning Jack was awake at the crack of dawn running round the cottage squeaking for all he was worth, with the result that he woke everyone up, and as there was no getting back to sleep after that; there was nothing for it but to get up, rather grumpily all round it must be said.

Jack repeated this performance the next morning and that evening when he was asleep Aunt Mary sneaked Bunny away from his tight embrace and hid it with the intention of giving it to him next morning at a more reasonable hour. But Jack, waking at the first sign of light as usual, and finding no Bunny beside him let out such a loud and anguished howl that we all jumped out of bed in fright wondering what had happened to him, and Bunny had to be produced immediately to still his cries.

The following morning all was peace and quiet and as we were sitting down to breakfast Jack came in looking very woebegone and holding up Bunny said "Poor Bunny's got no squeak any more" and he squeezed and squeezed with no result, and all that day he went around squeezing Bunny and looking puzzled and unhappy.

That evening as we were saying the prayers as usual Gran came to "God Bless Uncle Ned" and Jack pursed his lips tightly together and would not say a word.

"God Bless Uncle Ned, Jack" said Gran again.

"No" said Jack "I won't say 'God Bless Uncle Ned'. He's naughty! He took the squeak out of Bunny."

"How do ye know he did?" asked Gran.

"I heard him tell Aunt Mary" said Jack. "She's naughty too! She laughed when he told her, so I won't say 'God Bless Aunt Mary either' " and big tears rolled down his little face as he sobbed. "I liked it when Bunny squeaked!"

"There, there, agradh" said Gran. "Uncle Ned'll put the squeak back, won't ye Ned?"

Uncle Ned nodded. "But ye can only play with Bunny during the day and take Teddy to bed with ye like before. Will ye do that, Jack?"

Jack nodded and trotted off to bed with Gran but he was not ready to forgive yet because neither Uncle Ned nor Aunt Mary got a goodnight kiss that night.

More About Jack

We were all gathered round the kitchen table one morning, my mother, Gran and Aunt Mary enjoying a nice cup of tea, and Jack and I with a large cup of cold buttermilk each, when Uncle Ned came into the kitchen and said "Queenie is having her pups at last." Jack and I jumped up in great excitement clamouring to go and see them.

"No, not yet" replied Uncle Ned, "ye'll only disturb her. I'll let ye know when ye can. Don't go near her now until I say so, will ye?"

We promised we would not, and waited with as much patience as we could muster until next day when Uncle Ned said we could come and have a little peep.

"How many are there?" asked Gran.

"Well, now, that I can't say for sure" said Uncle Ned "about ten or eleven I think. They were wrigglin' about so much I couldn't be sure that I didn't count a couple twice. I'll have another go now with Jen to help me."

When we entered the kennel Queenie was curled round her little ones very protectively, and though she was very tired she managed a few welcoming wags of her tail.

We went nearer to have a closer look and Uncle Ned said to me "Now, Jen, as I put the little pups in this corner, try and stop them from wrigglin' back to Queenie so I can count thim properly."

17

B

I did my best to do so and quite a job it was. I was amazed at the sheer determination of those blind, feeble little bodies to get back to the warmth and sustenance of their mother. Queenie looked rather anxious during these proceedings, but Uncle Ned talked to her reassuringly all the while. "There, there me auld beauty. Shure an' we wouldn't harm yer little ones for the world."

We counted eleven pups.

When Uncle Ned had seen that all the pups were back to the warmth and protection of Queenie's body he patted her head and said "Well done, auld girl!" and Queenie looked up at him with her large brown eyes full of trust and affection. "We'll go now and leave her in peace" said Uncle Ned.

When we returned to the kitchen Uncle Ned said to Gran. "Yes, there are eleven all right."

"She'll never manage to feed thim all herself" said Gran. "Can ye get a foster mother to help out?"

"Old man Riley did tell me yesterday that his collie had just had pups. Mebbe he'll let us have her for a few weeks" said Uncle Ned.

The following morning Uncle Ned set off to see if Farmer Riley would loan the collie to us to help rear the pups for the first few weeks. I should mention here that Queenie was a brindle and white greyhound, and her litter of pups were quite valuable as the breeding was good. Soon Uncle Ned returned with the collie and her own three little pups, and when he had settled them down in an adjacent kennel to Queenie, but quite separate of course, he said he would leave her there for a day or so to get used to him before transferring a few of Queenie's pups to her.

So a couple of days later Uncle Ned came to me and said "I'm going now to clean out the kennels, Jen, and then I'll make a big bowl of grub for each of thim, an' while they're distracted with the food, ye can come and help me with the pups."

He was back in the kitchen almost immediately and he said to Gran "Ye won't believe this. I can hardly believe it meself. Queenie has eaten two of her own pups!" We all gasped in horror.

"Oh, Ned," said Gran "are ye sure? How do ye know?"

"It's true enough" said Uncle Ned. "I saw a few grisly little remains as I was sweepin' up so I vomited her to make sure."

We all sat in shocked silence for a little while and then Uncle Ned said "Well, I suppose I better get on with the grub, then ye can come out to give me a hand, Jen."

I still sat disbelieving that Queenie my lovely, gentle, affectionate Queenie, could do such a thing, and close to tears I said to Gran. "It just can't be true, can it Gran?" Gran put her arm round me. "Hush, child," she said "our ways are not Nature's ways. Queenie goes by her instincts, and mebbe her instincts told her she would niver be able to rear such a large litter properly. There was a reason for what she did, of that ye can be shure, if we only knew what it was!"

Soon Uncle Ned appeared at the half-door to the kitchen and beckoned me, and I went out to the kennel with him. He had a little box with a layer of straw in the bottom under his arm and he said to me. "Coax Queenie out with the bowl of soup, Jen, and I'll put three of the pups in the box while she's eatin' it."

This I did, and then we repeated this manoeuvre with the collie, and Uncle Ned added the three pups from Queenie to the three collie pups.

"Won't she know they're not hers?" I asked.

"No, Jen" he said "she goes on their scent and once they're all mixed up together she'll accept them as her own. It's lucky for us she can't count, isn't it? he said with a grin.

The next few weeks were happy and exciting ones for Jack and me as we were allowed to accompany Uncle Ned each time he went to feed Queenie and the collie, which soon became a great favourite also, and which we named Susie, and the delight of seeing the pups growing stronger and more playful each day soon put the unpleasant thought of the other two little casualties out of our minds.

Then one morning as Gran and I were in the kitchen we heard Aunt Mary loudly scolding a bawling Jack and in she came dragging him none too gently after her by the scruff of the neck.

"What's up, May?" asked Gran.

"This little divil was in Queenie's kennel, on his own, where he knows he oughtn't to be, and guess what he was doin'? Lickin' the pups lickin' thim no less!"

"God bless and save us" cried Gran in horror "that child will be the death of us all. There's just no knowin' what he'll get up to next."

"Well Queenie does it" bawled a bewildered Jack.

Gran got a cup, filled it with warm water, added a good spoonful of salt and made the protesting Jack drink until it had the desired effect.

When Uncle Ned came in Gran told him the story and she sighed "Childer will be childer, I suppose, but ye better keep that top bolt on in future."

"Aye, I will" said Uncle Ned. "So poor ole Jack's in the doghouse, so to speak, is he?" he said grinning.

"Now, stop that, Ned" said Gran wrathfully. "Lord only knows what horrible thing he could pick up, and if he'd got a hair stuck in his throat he could've choked in no time. So it's no laughin' matter!"

"I know that well" said Uncle Ned, glancing sympathetically at the very chastened but still uncomprehending Jack "still an' all" he tailed off and deciding that discretion was the better part, beat a hasty retreat as Gran cried "Arrah Ned, ye've no more sense yerself than the child here!"

The pups were a mixture of colours. There were brindle and white ones, fawns, plain brindles, a white with fawn spots, and one blue, and it was inevitable that we should each pick a favourite. Jack loved the little blue dog best, but I chose a little bitch, the one that resembled Queenie herself most, with a white head and neck, brindle body and four little white socks; and as they grew stronger, and their legs got longer, she was always the first to jump down from the wooden bed, covered in clean, fresh straw, which was raised slightly off the ground, and come to the door to greet us.

"Ah, there ye are as usual" said Uncle Ned stooping to play with her as she pranced delightedly round us. "A right auld cutie ye are, aren't ye, a right auld cutie."

And that's what we called her, Cutie. Cute she was, both in looks and by nature. She was always the leader, into every mischief, with the others running pell-mell after her. Uncle Ned had a fair sized paddock, enclosed by chicken wire, rigged up so that they could exercise in safety in the open air, or just lie on the grass sunning themselves, but while the others were playing or sleeping, Cutie would be prowling the fence looking for a spot to escape, and when she found it, she soon scooped an opening and was out and away looking for adventure. The others soon followed.

The poor old chickens had to flee squawking in all directions, nothing within reach was left on the line; she made off with Gran's doormat and with each one pulling and tugging it was soon reduced to shreds; and once she ventured right into the kitchen, seized a corner of the table-cloth and away with her leaving a pile of smashed crockery in her wake.

Uncle Ned was in constant hot water but as fast as he closed one escape route she opened another. What happy days they were and though I knew that Uncle Ned would probably sell all the pups, I hoped desperately that he would keep Cutie, but in any case by the time they were ready to go, Jack and I would be back in our own home in Glasgow, so I pushed that unpleasant thought out of my mind.

Jack's best friend was a little lad called Dominic Delaney who lived a few doors away, and, of course, the pups were a great lure to Dominic also, so that he was always about the place during the holidays. Dominic had blue eyes, flaming red hair, a round face smothered in freckles and an every ready grin. He was about eight years old, and on Sundays, Dominic was to be seen serving Mass, completely transformed in his snowy surplice, hair well plastered into some sort of order, solemn faced and eyes demurely downcast; and Jack's own eyes were glued to his every move.

We were all sitting down to Sunday dinner when Jack turned to Gran and said "Why didn't Dominic bring in the biscuits, Gran?"

"What biscuits?" asked Gran.

"The ones Father keeps asking him to bring in" said Jack.

"I don't know what ye mane" said Gran. "I niver heerd Father ask Dominic to bring anny biscuits."

"Yes he did Gran" said Jack "he asked Dominic three or four times, so why didn't he bring them in?"

Gran shook her head mystified as we all were. Enlightenment came the following Sunday as I saw Jack tug

Gran's sleeve and saw her put her arm round him in an affectionate hug as Father Rafferty turned round to the congregation, extended his arms and in a clear voice pronounced the words "Dominus Vobiscum."

After we had happily helped Uncle Ned to feed the pups we had our tea and then he said we could go with him to one of Farmer Riley's fields, where he had taken grazing for a few weeks, to bring home his two young heifers. It was about a half mile walk down a shady narrow lane, and when we came to the gate we espied the two heifers at the far end of the long field.

Uncle Ned cut us a switch each from the hedge and said "Here ye are, the pair of ye can bring up the heifers while I have a rest for meself."

We set off eagerly and soon had the two rounded up and on the way back at a brisk trot with Jack using his switch to good effect if either got sluggish.

Suddenly Uncle Ned appeared shouting angrily at us to "Take it aisy there. What d'ye mane by whackin' the heifers that way? Gimme that switch" grabbing it out of Jack's hand.

Jack was furious and sulked all the way home where he immediately ran to Gran to tell his tale of woe. When Uncle Ned came in Gran asked him what had happened.

"Ah, shure they had the heifers runnin' all over the place, and thim due to calve anny day. Whackin' thim he was with the switch."

"Well" said Jack with devastating four-year-old logic "if you didn't want me to use the switch, what did you give it to me for?"

Uncle Ned scratched his head ruefully. "Now there ye have me, old son" he said, "what did I give it to ye for indade?"

"Come on, Jack" said Gran, "I think it's time for bed little man. Ye've surely had a busy day haven't ye?"

Maryhill

It had been decided, to my great joy, that I could stay on for a few more weeks with Gran, and that Aunt Mary would accompany me back to Maryhill. Doodle Riley had promised to take my mother, and a very annoyed Jack, who wanted to be left also, to the local railway station in the pony and trap. Doodle was somewhat late in arriving and we were all sitting around rather on edge waiting for her to put in an appearance. It was not a very good day, showery and blustery, and my mother who was a poor sailor, was not looking forward to the journey one little bit. She had been put even more out of humour a little earlier when, having dressed Jack in a new jumper she had knitted during our stay, and his best brown corduroy pantaloons, she bade him sit still and wait whilst she got ready herself; Jack however could not bear to go off without one more farewell to Queenie and the pups, and came flying out to the yard where Uncle Ned and I were pottering about whiling away the waiting time, and as we watched in consternation, knowing what was about to happen but unable to stop Jack in full flight, he slipped and fell flat on his face in the mud.

"Oh, lor" said Uncle Ned "now we'll be for it."

He helped Jack up and surveyed the damage. Jack had a panel of mud from his neck to his toes but skipped along beside Uncle Ned quite unconcerned until he came to the window of the kitchen, when he suddenly broke out into a very loud and woeful bawling which brought Gran, Aunt Mary and my mother running to see what had happened. My mother was fit to be tied, of course, and waded into the three of us in no uncertain fashion, and Jack was hauled into the kitchen and washed and dressed in another outfit with my mother complaining that he would arrive looking like a ragbag. Gran tried to soothe things over by maintaining that it was only a little bit of mud and that she would soon get it out and send them back with Aunt Mary as good as new.

I can see Jack now in my mind's eye in his jumper and pantaloons. The bottom of the pantaloons were cut to give a spatlike effect with a bit of elastic to go under the foot to keep them neat. His jumper was of the natural oatmeal like colour with a wide panel of what was supposed to be Fair Isle pattern round the middle. My mother knitted all Jack's little suits, but always in plain stitch, but this time had determined to try and emulate the Scots housewives, who, of course, were great knitters, and produce something a little more elaborate. So she had bought a pattern and several balls of different coloured wool and set to. She soon found herself getting in a tangle with the several balls and roped me in to help, very unwillingly on my part I can tell you, as it was very tedious going, and I soon got my comic, and with one eye on that, and one on the pattern, I got very confused and instead of calling out two blue, I'd say, two white, or maybe one red, or what have you, with the result that a very weird pattern indeed emerged; and although my mother surveyed it very doubtfully from time to time, we carried on regardless. So Jack's jumper was truly unique. Jack hated those knitted pants, and his greatest wish in life was to have a pair of "proper trousers with pockets in".

Doodle duly arrived, and with more tears all round, they eventually set off with Uncle Ned going along to help them with the bags and get them settled on the train.

The next three weeks passed very quickly and soon it was time also for me to say farewell to Gran, Grandfather, Uncle Ned, Queenie and her pups, especially my own favourite little Cutie. I was very sad at leaving as usual, but soon got over it once we were on our way. Aunt Mary was happy too, she was looking forward to her holiday. There was plenty of social life, dances and whist drives, trips and sports' days, all of which she relished.

We did not have quarters in the Barracks itself, but had a very nice flat outside in a rather posh neighbourhood. The army leased several of these flats for NCOs if they had no suitable accommodation inside the Barracks, and the other tenants took rather a dim view of it — lowered the tone of the place in their opinion no doubt. This attitude always infuriated my mother who considered we were the equal, indeed superior, to quite a few of them. Her contempt was mostly concentrated on one tenant in our block, a loud-mouthed, flashily dressed man, whom she always maintained was a bookie — in my mother's view, quite the lowest form of animal life. Plenty of money, of course, and why wouldn't he, considering the easy way he got it, she would say. I heartily agreed with my mother's views. In my opinion there was not a man in the whole of Maryhill, let alone Carnegie Crescent, who could hold a candle to my father when he went out dressed in his black Glengarry, black jacket and tartan trews.

Although my father was in a Scottish Regiment he was not a Scot, but came from the Midlands of England. He, and his elder brother, my Uncle Percy, joined up together a few months before the outbreak of the First World War. I never heard him talk about it apart from a remark he made once when we were discussing preparations for a big party on the occasion of a close relative's twenty-first birthday and I asked him how he had spent his, and he had replied briefly that he had "celebrated" it in the trenches, and on another occasion many years later when Hannah invited home a young German she had met when he was on a visit to her firm, and he and my father had a long discussion about the war. He told us that at the age of fourteen he was drafted into an anti-aircraft battery and had to leave his home in Bavaria and go to a large town which was undergoing heavy air raids. At the age of sixteen he was called up and had to join the Submarine Service without being given any choice whatever in the matter.

He was intensely interested in the First World War, and listened avidly to my father's stories, especially to the tale of that football match which took place one Christmas on "no man's land" between a British team and a German team. Then there was the tale of the "Angel of Mons". As far as I can remember it went something like this. The Allies were routed and in full retreat; the men had to march for three days and nights without rest to avoid capture, and many spoke afterwards of the appearance of an angel beckoning and encouraging them whenever they felt too exhausted to carry on marching.

My father delighted that young man by telling him of one Christmas he remembered when they were faced by a Bavarian Regiment in the opposite trenches, and how they had called out greetings and sang carols together until it was put a stop to by an influx of Prussian Officers. He went right through from beginning to end — was in the retreat from Mons, won the Military Medal, and towards the end in 1918 was wounded in the head. He was operated on, and a silver plate was inserted in his temple. Many, many years later this plate showed up on an X-ray and the doctors expressed amazement at the great skill with which the very delicate operation had been performed, saying it could not be bettered even now.

The two brothers served together for some time until an unexpected incident separated them. A big recruitment drive was to be mounted in my father's home town and the two brothers were to lead a big parade at which they were to be presented with their medals; the Military Medal in my father's case; and the Distinguished Conduct Medal in Uncle Percy's. On his way to the parade however, Uncle Percy stuck his head out of the carriage window of the train and his Glengarry blew off and was lost for ever. He could not parade without his cap so just did not turn up at all. In fact, he never went back to his old regiment but joined up in another under an assumed name.

I have often wondered just how he got away with that, but get away with it he did, despite the fact that the Redcaps would turn up at his home from time to time enquiring for him, because, technically of course, he was a deserter. On one occasion the powers-that-be even put my father in charge of a squad detailed to pick him up and he persuaded them to let him go in first alone on the pretext of wishing to avoid a rough-house, which from all accounts Uncle Percy was very capable of kicking-up, and as he entered the front door, loudly proclaiming his presence and purpose, Uncle Percy smartly nipped out the back door.

Uncle Percy, of course, never got his medal which was a source of regret to him, as apart from the medal itself there was also a small annual cash entitlement attached to it which would have amounted to something quite considerable over the years as Uncle Percy was in his late eighties when he died.

My father left school when he was twelve. He had reached the fourth grade and that was as high as he could go. His father, who was a Master Baker by trade, suffered very poor health from a lung disease, most probably caused by his work, and the family were badly hit when he was laid up ill. So he just took what jobs he could get until he joined up, and when he got the King's Shilling, he left eight pence a day of it with his mother to help with the younger ones. He and Grandmother used to laugh together when they sang the old song substituting the words "all for fourpence a day" for "a shilling a day" as they sang it together.

He stayed in the army after the war making it his career. Although he served at various army camps throughout England, I have no recollection of them apart from two incidents which I do barely remember. One was of somehow getting hold of some scissors and chopping off all my curls which were my parents' chief pride, and my chief asset.

Gran often told me also of the beautiful hair I had "the colour of a new penny" she said it was, and how after I had created havoc with it, cutting it all bits and pieces, it never grew curly again.

The second incident was when I and a little playmate somehow escaped from under my mother's usually watchful eye and wandered off. We were gone all day, causing consternation, with the whole regiment out looking for us. We were eventually brought home by a young gypsy man who used to sell wooden pegs, mats, artificial flowers and the like, who remembered seeing us earlier when my mother had bought some little thing from him. We had wandered quite a long way from home and were barely able to put one foot in front of the other we were so tired.

Before Maryhill we were at Wishaw where my father was in charge of the Territorials. We had a nice house and there was a big hall where we used to play if it was wet. My father became something of a hero there because of an incident at the local cattle market when a bull broke loose and went on the rampage through the streets, and he was called upon to shoot it which he did with one shot right in the centre of the forehead. I knew nothing about it until I went to school and my schoolmates were full of it telling me how my father had knelt down in the path of the charging bull and with one shot it went down as if poleaxed. I, of course, revelled in the reflected glory. He was an excellent shot representing the regiment many times at Bisley.

My mother met my father soon after the end of the First World War. She had not long recovered from a severe attack of the influenza which took such a terrible toll of the country. She lost all her hair, her beautiful hair, which she was the only one of the family to inherit from my grandmother, and she told me of how Gran used to sneak into the darkened room and gather up the hair from the pillow, hiding it away from her in case she should worry about it, but although she was aware of what was going on she was too ill to care. When her hair grew once more it was thick and glossy as ever but she never let it grow again as short bobbed hair was then the fashion.

My father was already a Sergeant which was considered a good match. He progressed in the course of time to Company Sergeant-Major but he knew he would not get any of the "plum" jobs such as Regimental Sergeant-Major because he was too small. He was only five feet six inches. My mother told me she got a shock the first time she saw my father drilling the men; she could not believe the strength of his voice; he was always so soft-spoken otherwise. My mother was the absolute mistress in our house and the only time I can remember seeing my father in a real rage was once when Jack and I got into a bad-tempered fight together when he pulled us apart and spanked us both. My mother loved the dances, the skirl of the pipes, the swing of the kilts, the sword dancing and the accompanying wild Highland yells. My father was a fair bit of a boxer and she told me once that one night at a dance the Regimental champion, who also had a bit of an eye for her, spent quite a large slice of the evening telling her just what he was going to do to him when they met in a forthcoming bout. He was as good as his word but though he kept knocking my father down he kept bouncing back like a rubber ball, and soon the whole hall was behind him vociferously egging him on with the lone voice of my mother screaming out to him to stay down. She was afraid that some serious damage could occur because of the wound in his temple. He was carried out in triumph shoulder high as though he had won.

My father's company always had the lowest recorded "crime" in the Regiment and once he was called in before the top brass to explain why this was so. I do not know what he said but I have no doubt myself that my father turned many a blind eye rather than put any raw young rookie on "report".

There was another incident which I always found rather intriguing, which happened before they were married. It appears there was some trouble over a girl and one of the men, and local feeling was running very high at the time. One evening there was a soft knock at the door and a woman's voice asked to speak to my grandmother. When she came to the door she saw a woman, dressed in black, who kept in the shadow with her shawl closely held over her head and face. She said she had come to warn the family because she had heard some of the men planning some sort of retaliation and that one of them had said "Nan Fitzroy is going with one of them, we could get him one night! Just tell him to be on his guard" she said. My grandmother thanked her and she melted away into the night. They never found out who she was, but nothing ever came of it.

It was whilst we were in Wishaw that I have my first memory of travelling back from holiday with Aunt Mary. She was not expected, which was not an unusual occurrence with my Aunt Mary who was a law unto herself and would just pack up and leave at once if she took the notion to do so. At any rate when we arrived there was no one at home. Nothing daunted, she lifted me up to get through an open window and was just about to climb in herself when a heavy hand descended on her shoulder and she turned in fright to see the largest policeman she had ever seen in her life who said something in such a broad Scots accent that she could not understand a word, but guessing what it was all about, launched into a torrent of explanations herself, which judging from the expression on his face, the policeman found equally unintelligible. Luckily my mother appeared soon after with Jack whom she had taken for a walk and everything was cleared up.

I suppose Aunt Mary would have been about nineteen at the time, and I realise now that she was quite a resourceful young lady considering the much more "kept down" attitude adopted to women in those days. Not that Aunt Mary was in the least "kept down", she had far too much spirit for that. She had travelled over for the first time when she was barely seventeen. It was the time when Jack was born and she came to look after me whilst my mother was away in the hospital. My father was to meet her at the boat, but as luck would have it, he was late, and as Aunt Mary had been given strict instructions to stay on the boat until he arrived, this she did, getting more and more agitated as everyone left until she was alone on deck with her few bits and pieces. She was joined by a very elegant lady, swathed in furs, who was most sympathetic and told her not to worry in the least, that she had transport and would be only too pleased to see that she got home safely. Aunt Mary was just about to get into the large car when my father arrived and in the flurry both lady and car quickly disappeared. They were joined by two men who said they were plain clothes policemen who proceeded to question Aunt Mary closely as to every word the elegant lady had said to her. On being asked what it was all about they said they were enquiring into the disappearance a few weeks ago of a young girl who, like Aunt Mary, had travelled over alone for the first time. She was known to have left the boat in the company of a very elegant lady and had not been seen or heard of since. They expressed the opinion that Aunt Mary had had a very lucky escape, but as my father said to my mother later, in his opinion it was the elegant lady who had had the narrow escape. As I have said my Aunt Mary was very headstrong and no one had been able to make her do anything she did not want to do since the day she was born.

It was in Wishaw also that an incident happened that I have always remembered in every detail. I was fond of my Aunt Mary and usually we got on very well together, but this day we had a violent disagreement. I must tell you here that soon after Aunt Mary was born she had developed an ulcer on her leg. The doctors had wished to amputate but Gran would not hear of it, and begged them to do anything but that. So they had cut out the affected part but the leg never grew properly after, it was slightly shorter and thinner than the other one. I do not remember what the disagreement was about, I only remember screaming out "Go home, go home to your own house, old long leg, short leg." I can vividly remember the shocked silence in the room and the look on Aunt Mary's face before she recovered herself and passed it off with a laugh. I did not realise then the very real distress the disability caused Aunt Mary, I had only wanted to hurt and young as I was I knew I had, deeply, and I felt a sense of shame which has remained with me to this day. The incident was never mentioned again but all through the years I remained in contact with Aunt Mary and I tried to make amends in little ways and always made allowances for her even when she was at her most trying, and trying she could certainly be. She was never mean, she was generous with what she had and God knows that was very little all through her life.

Aunt Mary stayed with us in Maryhill all that winter thoroughly enjoying the social scene. That Christmas was a memorable one for Jack, he at last got those "proper trousers with pockets in" he so much wanted and we also got a new baby sister, Hannah. Hannah was a lovely child taking after my father's side of the family with dark hair and brown eyes, and she was very quiet. She had only one fault in my eyes, she was very hard to get off to sleep and that was my job rocking the cradle until she did go off. I always had a book, of course, but as the days lengthened I wanted to be out with my friends who would be calling for me, and I would be in a fever of impatience, rock, rocking away vigorously until I thought I could escape, tiptoeing away, only for her to open one eye and then her little mouth to yell, bringing me back hotfoot.

The flats formed a square round a concreted area for the use of the residents where we could play in safety and Hannah would be put out there in the fresh air in her pram in my charge. The previous year Jack had been given a long wooden snake for Christmas. It was cut in sections which when he pulled it along behind him gave a quite realistic semblance of wriggling. To begin with it had been beautifully painted, but over the course of time and very hard use, as Jack never went out without it, it had lost nearly all its paint, but Jack did not mind, and continued his ceaseless parading, but now with an added swagger, one hand stuck in the pocket of his new trousers. There was one little girl in the block of flats of whom I had always been rather envious, she possessed something I would dearly have liked to own — a fairy cycle. She had no brothers or sisters, though, and was fascinated by Hannah, and I would graciously allow her to wheel her about in her pram for the loan of the fairy cycle.

We seemed to have seasons for different games, skipping, spinning our tops, running with our wooden hoops, or walking on our "stilts" which we made by boring two holes in old tin cans and passing rope through the holes. Everything would be put away and brought out again next "season".

In the winter we had other pastimes. We each bought a different comic and exchanged, and we had cardboard cut out dolls for which you could buy cardboard "outfits", but we also made our own copying the styles from the magazines and papers. I was especially attracted by the costumes of the ladies of medieval times and would spend countless happy hours drawing and colouring the dresses. Then we had scraps. Scraps came in sheets, lovely glossy cut outs joined together by little tags, of animals, birds, butterflies, insects, all mixed up together, and we had albums to put them in and would exchange with one another to try to get the set.

The undisputed highlight of our week, however, was the Saturday morning visit to the pictures. If we missed an episode of the serial it was deprivation on a grand scale, and we could scarcely contain our impatience as we waited to see how the heroine made her escape from the terrible fate only seconds away.

Every Friday there was a twenty mile route march and, of course, we would all assemble to watch as it passed our road, led by the pipes and drums, the lilting music putting new life into the weary men as they turned into the barracks, and we would wait for my father to fall out.

Friday was pay day and we would get our three pence, riches indeed! It was one penny to get into the pictures, silent of course. The "talkies" had arrived, but it was tuppence to get into them. You could get quite a lot for a ha' penny, a bag of aniseed balls, liquorish pipes, gob-stoppers. We liked those, they were all different colours in layers, and we would have a good suck and then have a look to see what colour it was then have another suck and repeat the performance. Bubble gum was another favourite, and then there was that lovely gooey toffee which came in trays with a little hammer that the shopkeeper used to break it up into small pieces; enough to give you lockjaw too, as it would stick both sets of teeth firmly together if you were not careful.

There was a very extensive and beautiful Botanical Gardens at the foot of our road, and that is where we spent most of our time. I marvel now at the complete freedom we had to roam. On the rare occasions when I could get out without Jack or Hannah of a summer evening, my friend Betty, who lived underneath us, and I would position ourselves near the ice-cream seller at the entrance to the park with wistful expressions, and it worked too; many a cornet we got from people who would be buying for themselves. Then we would find out if there were any weddings due to take place in the vicinity and make sure we were there to join in the scramble for the handfuls of small change which were always thrown to the assembled kids.

Times were very hard for a great many people then and, although, of course, we were relatively affluent and lived in a prosperous part, still I was aware of the fact that others were not so fortunate. I remember always feeling a little bit apprehensive — why I do not know — when I had to pass the large groups of unemployed men who used to congregate on the street corners. "Corner boys" they were rather unkindly called, thin and hungry looking with cloth caps and a muffler round their necks. Then there were the ex-Servicemen, selling their matches, or perhaps playing, four or five together, in a band, and we used to roll up a few pence in newspaper and throw it down to them, in company with most of our

c

neighbours. There was one set of people for whom my father always had the highest regard, and that was the Salvation Army, and would never pass them by without dropping something in their collecting box. He never forgot their efforts to alleviate the misery of the troops during the war.

Sunday was deadly. None of our friends were allowed out. The only place open was the museum, and we were well known there I can tell you. Sunday after Sunday Jack and I would spend hours wandering round.

In the summer there were sports' days in the barracks, gymkhanas, trips down the Clyde to Rothesay and Dunoon. In the winter we had the Christmas Party to look forward to, and what super presents we got. There were often large fairs locally and we would always go, with my father insisting on taking us on most of the rides to our great joy. My father on the 'cakewalk', especially if he had a pint or two inside him, was something to see I can tell you. We would come home with armfuls of prizes he would win at the shooting galleries.

We loved it when my mother went into Glasgow shopping. My father would make the tea, everything arranged very daintily — bread wafer thin, and lashings of butter; a delicious omelette or scrambled eggs, and everything he could find put out on the table; and did we tuck in! When my mother returned she would eye the empty larder and no doubt think to herself it was a good job she did not go shopping very often for the sake of the household budget at any rate.

My father always went to the whist drives, and always won something. It was only very rarely that my mother could be persuaded to accompany him, she was too nervous about leaving us alone. And she had good reason to be nervous too, did she but know it. We were all put into the one bedroom, bribed to be good by comics and chocolate, and Jack and I promised everything we were asked to promise; but as soon as we were reasonably sure that they had really gone (it was quite likely that my mother would change her mind and come home again almost as soon as she had left), we leapt out of bed and ran to the kitchen where I immediately set about making pancakes which I had learned to do at our cookery classes at school, and Jack and I would feast together delightedly.

Then Jack and I would sit as quiet as we could in the hope

that our little pet, a mouse, would put in an appearance. We loved the little creature, he was so timid that it was not easy to entice him out even though we sprinkled little titbits for him thus completely circumventing my mother's strenuous efforts to get rid of him. She would scrupulously sweep up every crumb saying "Well, he won't get anything to eat in my kitchen anyway. And how did he get in? Four flights up, you'd think we'd be safe from them!" I had no fear of him. He knew where his home was and never strayed far from it, not like the field-mice at Gran's where I never knew where they would pop out from; perhaps from under the cushion of the chair I was just about to sit on, or from under the bed narrowly missing my bare feet causing me to hop in even quicker than I usually did.

Then we would clear up, oblitering every single trace of our escapade, so much so that my mother never had the slightest suspicion. How we managed that I do not know. It was not as though my mother was an unobservant person, she was anything but, and she was absolutely horrified many years later when we told her, and indeed I am horrified myself now when I think what could have happened, considering I had to stand on a chair to turn on and light the gas mantle for a start.

We had an old gramophone which we loved although it was quite a chore continuously changing the needle and winding it up, and we had all the popular records. We had the "Laughing Song" which always made us laugh as well; we had "Tiptoe thru' the Tulips"; "The Sun has got its Hat on"; my father's favourite "Lily of Laguna"; and "The Campbells are coming, Hurrah, Hurrah". Jack was not in the least musical, his main interest was in putting small objects on the turntable and endeavouring to catch them as they flew off. But one day he said casually to my father, "Why were they so glad the camels were coming, Dad?" which made my father laugh and exclaim, "Well, that's a good one, Jack! I must remember to tell that one in the mess tonight" before launching into the tale of the beleagured garrison in some far-flung outpost of Empire, in dire straits and on the point of surrendering, when they heard the wail of the bagpipes in the distance heralding the arrival of the relief column. Jack was impressed and thereafter joined enthusiastically in the "Hurrahs" with the rest of us.

It was on one of those afternoons when my mother had gone shopping that a disaster occurred. We broke her favourite record "Ramona". I think it was actually my father who broke it, but we all entered into the conspiracy of silence and sat in fear and trepidation thereafter on the quite frequent occasions when my mother would want it played and started hunting through the pile, never finding it of course, and muttering to herself that she must have lent it to someone, and now who could it be? She never suspected what had happened. In fact my mother was a singularly unsuspicious person.

We had a little dairy-cum-bakery-cum-general provision shop round the corner, and we used to get delicious baked-that-morning baps delivered with the milk for breakfast. Many a time I would be despatched for a quarter of fresh ham for sandwiches and I would be unable to resist having a little pick here and there, with the result that I would arrive back with considerably less than a quarter, and she would survey it angrily and say "That's a very scutty quarter, a proper robber that fellow is! I've a good mind to take it back and have it out with him!" I would be terrified, but she never did, and I would forget my terror and do the same thing the next time, and many a farthing or, more daringly, a ha'penny, I purloined to boot.

I would do exactly the same thing when I was sent for fish and chips, I would help myself all the way home. Talking of chips reminds me of another episode which did me no credit. Several times as I wandered round the barracks of an evening I would be hailed by some young rookie and asked if I would go for a portion of fish and chips for him. The fish shop was outside the barracks, so perhaps they were confined to barracks for some reason. Anyway the money would be duly handed through the window and on delivering the fish and chips I would receive a penny for my trouble. One evening when this happened I did not go back, temptation proved too strong, I just kept the poor lad's sixpence for myself.

Jack was always what my mother called a "rooter" which means that he was forever rooting through the larder in his quest for something to eat. He was especially fond of meat and many a half-eaten joint destined for the next day's dinner disappeared down Jack's gullet. I was not averse to doing a bit of rooting myself but I went in search of sweet things. This sweet tooth was shared by my mother and on a Sunday especially we always had an extra nice cake for tea. I remember one occasion when we had a Battenburg cake and Aunt Mary did not eat her piece at the time but deposited it in the larder for later. I just could not resist that lovely almond icing and helped myself. Jack, of course, got the blame, no one heeding his vehement denials as he always denied he was the culprit anyway. Aunt Mary was furious but my mother gave her scant sympathy saying she should have eaten it at the proper time and not be putting temptation in the child's way.

We did not go to Gran's that year. One reason for that was that my father was nearing the end of his time in the army and would soon be leaving for good. The regiment was split — half of it always serving abroad, and my father's battalion was posted to India to relieve another battalion which had completed its tour of duty. It was decided that my father would accompany the men out on the troop-ship returning with the home-coming men. He did this twice and then, after some leave, was to attend a six month course in motor mechanics in the South of England which he hoped might prove useful in his search for a job.

In the meantime I had left my primary school at which I had been very happy and gone to a secondary, which I hated. It was very large and the standard was very high, and I had a job to keep up in most subjects — there were a couple — geometry and algebra, of which I never could make head nor tail. We had a young teacher just out of training college, anxious to make his mark no doubt, aggressive and impatient and a bit too ready to use the strap. I got many a lick of that strap, mainly for not knowing the answers to the questions. It did not hurt all that much, the hurt was more to the spirit in my case, the indignity of it. I remember there were a few of the hardier lads at the back of the class, from the poorer and tougher parts of the town, who would refuse to hold out their hands. The ringleader had a shock of dark hair, dark eyes, and a red pullover, which he wore constantly, threadbare at the elbows. There were several confrontations between him and the teacher. He was invariably late for class, and the teacher would make us all rise and call out "Good morning" to him when he did eventually put in an appearance; but he would only grin, not one whit abashed.

The only other teacher I remember was my form mistress. She was old, or maybe she was not, but viewed from my tender years, she was. She took us for music and history. She was a very large woman intensely proud of her Scots heritage, and I would listen enthralled to her tales of Wallace, Bruce and the Spider, and Flora MacDonald and Bonnie Prince Charlie. I can see her now as she bent to listen to each member of the class determined to find the one who was traitorously singing flat during the communal rendering of "Speed Bonnie Boat". I only stayed at that school a few months and I was very glad to leave.

Three impressions of Maryhill I have always retained. First, that of a warm-hearted people who really liked "bairns". Second, the neighbourhood policeman who, whenever he caught us in some minor misdemeanour; such as climbing over the dangerous spiked railings to the Botanical Gardens, or swinging on the lamp-posts; would make great play of getting out his notebook and taking down our names and addresses. We all gave false ones, which he knew full well, saying he had our names now and woe betide us if we ever did it again. Third, always being fascinated by the lamplighter especially on a cold, wet night, as he went from standard to standard with his pole with the hook on it to switch each one on, the street gradually lighting up as he went on his way.

"Is that a Bull over there?"

The following year we left Maryhill for good, and we all went to Gran's for the summer holiday as usual. It had been decided that when my father's leave was up he would travel to England to take his course, and then try to find a job and a house for us to live in; and, in the meantime, we would all stay with Gran.

The first thing Jack and I did, of course, after we arrived was to rush out to the yard to renew acquaintance with our beloved old Queenie, and when she saw us she came bounding towards us, tail wagging furiously in welcome. Then it was Cutie's turn, because Uncle Ned had kept her to replace Queenie as his brood bitch when Queenie became too old as he wished to retain the breeding. Bluey had gone, much to Jack's regret, but Uncle Ned had also kept a brindle dog, which had a couple of patches of white and, of course, we very unoriginally called him Spot.

Cutie and Spot were coming up to two years old, and Uncle Ned had decided to enter them for several of the local Coursing Meetings to be held during the winter, and he and Paddy Dooley, his friend, had arranged to take them over the fields to see if they could put up a hare to chase. He asked me if I would like to come. I, of course, said I would.

Accordingly, a couple of days later we set out. I took Cutie, Paddy took Spot, and Uncle Ned took Queenie, because he said she was an old hand at the game, still very alert and enthusiastic, and if there was a hare to be found, she was the

39

most likely one to see it. It was a nice warm morning, but Gran made me wear my wellies because it was damp underfoot, especially if we went through long grass. So we set off with Cutie excitedly hopping and jumping alongside me.

We had crossed a couple of fields without a sight of a hare and were well into another when Uncle Ned stopped suddenly and said to Paddy "Is that a bull over there?"

Paddy looked. "Begorrah it is an' all" he said.

"Here, Jen" said Uncle Ned "give Cutie to me and go back to the other field. Ye can make yer way round on the other side to join us later. Don't run and remember that it's only a very few that are wicked."

I handed him Cutie and started to walk away endeavouring to control my panic, but when I looked back and saw the bull lumber to his feet from amongst his wives where they had been resting in the shade of the hedge, I decided not to wait to find out if he was one of the few or not, and I broke into a headlong run for the hedge, somehow or other scrambling through with unbounded relief, heedless of the scratches and cuts I picked up in the process.

Of course the thought of meeting a bull was a constant nightmare to me but that was the closest I ever came, apart from one evening as Jack and I were strolling down the lane on our way to get the milk and Jack, as usual skipping on ahead around the bend, suddenly came flying back screaming "The bull, the bull, it's loose in the lane." The two of us took to our heels and did not stop until we were safely home. Luckily it appeared the bull was too busy trying to break into a field of young heifers to bother about anything else.

I had always known that one day we would run into that bull in the lane, but I had imagined that it would be one evening as he led his wives back to pasture after milking, and I was always wary despite the fact that the Rileys assured me that he was only a young bull and very docile. I had heard too many tales of hitherto docile bulls suddenly turning vicious and attacking their handlers.

Bullocks and cows too could be vicious. I remember Kathleen Riley telling me of how one day as she took her usual short cut home across a field one of the bullocks made an unexpected and vicious attack upon her, and she was lucky to get to the safety of a tree in the hedge, and there she had to stay with the furious bullock bellowing and butting the trunk until the commotion attracted the attention of some of the men who drove it off. Incidentally the bullock was one that had been hand reared by the young Rileys themselves, and it is said that these are the ones that most often turn vicious. I suppose they lose their fear of humans or something like that by virtue of being handled when calves.

Then Uncle Ned had a young cow that used to go absolutely berserk if he came into the field where she was with the dogs. He told us that one evening when he had temporarily overlooked the fact that she was in the field, and he was walking Spot and Cutie, she had made a determined effort to injure the two dogs. He said he had been fortunate to get out of the field without injury to himself or the dogs, which he had on the lead, and he knew he had to hang on to them at all costs. No easy task, they were big and strong, bucking and pulling, frantic with fear. If they had got away in their frightened state, heaven only knows what might have happened, they could easily have injured themselves, and as they represented quite an investment to Uncle Ned, he hung on for dear life. Many a time later on I used to get quite nervous when Uncle Ned and I were in an adjoining field galloping the two dogs, as she would be bellowing and running furiously up and down the hedge alongside us trying to break through. Uncle Ned said she was probably trying to protect him, as he milked her she likely thought of him as her calf.

Having gained the safety of the hedge I watched as Uncle Ned and Paddy made their way steadily and cautiously across the field, and breathed a sigh of relief when I saw that the bull stayed put and contented himself with watching them out of sight. It was lucky they had spotted him before they got too near or the outcome could have been very different. I made my way round and joined the other two in a large field bordering the road which, I was relieved to see, was unoccupied. We made our way as quietly as we could up the field when Queenie suddenly barked excitedly.

"She sees somethin' " said Uncle Ned. "Let thim go."

He slipped Queenie's collar, and we did the same for Cutie and Spot. The three took off at a furious pace with Uncle Ned and Paddy racing in pursuit.

"Stay here, Jen" called Uncle Ned "ye can pick thim up if they come back."

I stayed there and watched as the three dogs disappeared into the next field. In those days the fields were mostly small, one leading into another through gaps in the hedge which would be concealed until you were right on top of them. I waited there for quite a while with no sign of any of them, and was just about to make my way towards the place where they had all disappeared, when two large horses burst through the gap with the three dogs in hot pursuit and bore down at a furious gallop straight for me. I waited no longer, turned and ran for the low brick wall, took a flying leap across a muddy ditch, slipped and fell in getting my wellies full of mud and water, scrambled out and over the wall to the road. The dogs meanwhile had turned the horses again and were careering joyously back up the field, disappearing through the gap once more.

I emptied my wellies miserably and waited. I waited quite a while and then I decided to make my way home the long way via the road. Nothing would have made me go into that field again. I remembered vividly one occasion when Kathleen and I had been out looking for mushrooms and seeing a likely field we had warily looked to see if there were any potential hazards, and seeing none, we climbed in. We were in a field which was used for racehorses, we knew from the inner protective fence running all round, and we well knew that mares with foals, or worse still, a stallion, could be very dangerous indeed. Kathleen spotted it first and was off shouting to me and I saw a large black beast, which had not yet seen us, further down the field. Kathleen I am sure broke all records in that dash and I was a close second as we sprinted for the fence, crawled under and through the hedge, and as we raced on we could hear the animal snorting and bucking on the other side.

It was quite late in the afternoon when I eventually arrived home to find Uncle Ned was just about to set out in search of me having been there for some time. Gran, Aunt Mary and my mother surveyed me in silence for a few minutes and, indeed, I must have had that "pulled through a hedge backwards look", with a vengeance — filthy wellies, torn clothes, and full of scratches and cuts. Uncle Ned, as usual, got a blast from all three and he could only murmur lamely "Ah, shure, I only thought it'd be a little treat for her!"

Uncle Ned was only a few years older than me, and through the years I got him into hot water on several occasions. I would tag along after him all the time. Many times we mitched from school, a fact which he always says now he cannot remember, but I remember well. He had to take me with him of course and we would spend the day checking up on our birds' nests; making hidey-holes and dens in the gorse; drinking the ice-cold spring water, cupping it in our hands as it spurted up in a small steady jet; and eating our sandwiches. Then when we saw the other children on their way home, we would stroll in casually just as though we had been to school as usual. Gran did not suspect.

We were kindred spirits in that we would both read anything we could lay our hands on. His most prized possessions during his schooldays were the weekly boys' adventure booklets, and he had a little cupboard of his own where they were kept neatly stacked away. He would get very annoyed if I touched them, and would give me strict instructions to leave them alone, but of course, as soon as he had gone out I would make a bee-line for the cupboard. He would stay in bed as long as he could on a Saturday, and I remember one occasion when he called down to me to know what time it was. I called back "The big hand's at so and so and the little hand's at so and so." This caused my grandfather, who happened to be sitting in the kitchen having a cup of tea to exclaim, "D'ye mane to tell me, Jen, that ye can't tell the time properly yet?" I replied in the affirmative. "Come here, then, an' I'll show ye" he said, and this he proceeded to do, several times; but I still did not get the hang of it. "I only had to tell Ned once and he knew how" he said, to my utter mortification.

The weeks were flying by all too quickly and one day I told Gran that Kathleen wanted me to go mushroom picking with her as she knew of a good field, and it was quite safe as they only had a few calves in it. So Gran said I could go and handed me a little can to gather them in. I filled the can, and we had them for tea fried with bacon. There can be few things to compare with fresh field mushrooms, full of flavour, picked and eaten straight away.

During tea I told Gran about a little ring I had come across in the grass. It seemed to be burned or at least the grass had died leaving a circle.

"That's a fairy ring" said Gran, "I hope ye didn't step in it!"

"No, Gran, I didn't, but why shouldn't I?" I asked.

"Cos it's bad luck, agradh" said Gran. "The fairies were out dancin' last night, that's the sign, and they won't like it if ye go traipsin' all over it. Ye didn't hear a sound o' tappin' by anny chance did ye?" she asked.

"No, Gran, I didn't" I said. "Why?"

"Well" said Gran "if the little folk were out dancin' last night they very likely need either new shoes or their ole ones mended, so the little leprechaun'll have plenty of work to do. If ye do hear him at work, creep up on him from behind and grab holt of him, niver takin' yer eyes off him, 'cos if ye do he'll just vanish. He'll do everythin' he can to make ye look away, but if ye don't, and demand his purse, he'll have to give it to ye and there'll be a gold coin in it every time ye open it."

Gran seemed perfectly serious, so much so, indeed, that my father remarked "You don't really believe in leprechauns and fairies, do you Mam?"

"Ah, not atall" said Gran airily "I don't believe in thim atall."

Kathleen and I were to go out again first thing to get the pick of the mushrooms in the morning dew, and as Gran handed me the can she said "Bring some av the little button ones this time. Ye didn't bring anny yisterday an' they're the nicest."

"I thought I'd leave them to get bigger for this morning, Gran!" I said.

"Ah, shure, child" said Gran, "onst ye've put yer eye on thim they don't grow anny more, so ye may as well pick thim all, no matter how small."

As I set off Gran's parting words were "Keep an eye out for that leprechaun now. An' remember if ye see a fairy ring, don't step in it, as though we don't believe in thim, they're there just the same an' they'll be watchin' ye and they'll put a bad spell on ye if ye do!"

The Guard "Dog"

My father left soon after to go to England to take his course and then try and find a job and a house for us all to join him. It was about the same time too that change set in for Gran also, as Uncle Ned had bought a smallholding, a few acres, and a nice little bungalow; and on this particular day we were all up at the new place getting it shipshape. Aunt Mary, Gran, and my mother had strolled down to the little village drapers to see if they could get some curtain material. Uncle Ned was off somewhere too, leaving me there in charge of Jack and Hannah.

There was a knock on the door and I opened it to find a young man who said he had been on the road all day walking to such and such a place, which was still quite a few miles away, and could I give him a bite to eat and a cup of tea. I told him to sit outside on the garden seat and I would get it ready. We often got visitors like that "travellin' min" Gran called them, and she never refused the cup of tea and a little of whatever was going — maybe a bowl of stew if it was ready, or just a few slices of bread and butter. I think they must have told one another that they would be sure to get a "sup o' tay" at our place as we seemed to get more than our fair share; but be that as it may, there were two regular callers that I particularly remember. One was a thin little man who somehow managed to look neat in his shabby old clothes. He was well spoken, had very good manners and always presented Gran with a little gift

45

in appreciation — perhaps a thimble, a packet of darning needles or such like. Gran was rather intrigued by him as he certainly was not the usual run of the mill, and often wondered how he had come down in the world to such an extent, never questioning him of course. The other was a very big man who used to shamble quickly through the village, talking to himself and with the village kids, who always maintained that he plastered his hair with boot blacking, whistling and jeering after him.

I set about making the pot of tea and was just about to take it out when it started to rain quite heavily. The next minute the door opened and the young man came in and asked if he could sit inside as he was getting very wet. I did not know what to do so set the tea and bread and butter before him, and he ate hungrily, and as he ate he talked, and as he talked I got more and more anxious. He talked about his hard life and the harsh way he had always been treated. He talked about the way people would run him off their property, threatening him with sticks, or set the dogs on him, and once, he said, a farmer had chased him off with a hatchet. As I looked at him more closely I could see why the superstitious country folk ran him off, he had red hair and bright, unnaturally bright, blue eyes, one of which had a very pronounced squint, a combination which was supposed to bring bad luck. I gathered Jack and Hannah closer to me and my heart gave a sickening leap as he asked if I was alone, but I had the presence of mind to say no, that my uncle was at that moment in the garden digging a few spuds for the dinner and would be in soon. I jumped up quickly and said "There he is now." He leapt to his feet at once and was off, mumbling his thanks. Uncle Ned did indeed come in almost immediately afterwards and asked what he had wanted, as he thought he was acting very peculiarly, almost running down the road, continually looking back over his shoulder, and he had been worried when he saw him coming out of our gate. I have often thought of that young man, he was probably harmless, but truly one of life's unfortunates.

The incident rather worried Uncle Ned, though, and he said he would have to see about getting a good watch-dog for the times when Gran would be there alone; always supposing he could persuade her to leave the village at all. Gran had lived there for a very long time and loved company, and the new place was rather isolated even though it was on a main road. Aunt Mary was an upholsteress by trade, when she could get any to do, or rather she could get plenty to do but getting paid for it was another thing altogether. Then she sometimes did a little dressmaking, especially children's clothes, and a bit of "Skivvying" as she called it, when she could get it. She knew that she would have to go to Dublin if she wanted any sort of a permanent job.

It was a lovely evening and Aunt Mary said she would take a stroll and get the milk and Jack and I could come with her. So we set off and when we arrived at Riley's they were just sitting down to their supper and we were invited, of course, to have a cup with them. Mrs Riley set a cup and saucer before Aunt Mary, and just a cup for Jack and me with a large slice of apple tart for each of us. Jack looked at his cup and turned to Mrs Riley and asked very politely if he could have a saucer too. Mrs Riley obliged.

Then he said once more "Could I have a saucer to match my cup please, like I have at home."

Aunt Mary and I were rather embarrassed, but Mrs Riley only laughed good-naturedly, and rummaged in her cupboard until she came up with a matching saucer, which she duly put under his cup saying "There ye are, now, an isn't it the foine little gintleman ye are, to be shure!" Whereupon we all set to and there was no standing on ceremony in that house I can tell you.

Mrs Riley was a very large woman who always seemed to have a floury look and smell about her, as well she might. She baked all the bread her large family ate, and had a habit of putting the large round cakes out on the stone pillars of the gates to cool, and it was very seldom indeed that I passed Riley's without seeing the bread arranged on the pillars. It must have been quite a chore keeping them in bread.

That evening, after Jack had been put to bed and I was snug also in my bed in the kitchen listening to all the chat, Aunt Mary told the tale of Jack and the cup and saucer to my mother, Gran, and Uncle Ned who thought it a great joke and Aunt Mary said laughingly to my mother "Ye'll have to do somethin' about Jack, Annie, ye just can't take him anywhere."

"I know that well," said my mother, and she told how Jack,

when he was a little younger, used to dance with fury when a certain neighbour came to visit whom he disliked intensely for some reason, shouting at her to go home to her own house and would persist in spite of all the dire warnings, and indeed, many a smack.

Then there was the time that we had gone on an outing with the regiment and were all sitting down to lunch when Jack piped up "This meat's tough, isn't it, Mum?" unfortunately in a lull in the general conversation so that it carried to almost everyone. And in spite of my mother's frantic efforts to quieten him he had kept on, amidst several gasps of smothered laughter from the other tables; and how the colonel's lady had come up to us later and said that Jack was just like her own grandson, that she had always thought there could not be another like him in the world, but Jack was his equal.

"So, if you have any suggestions, I'll be only too glad to hear them" said my mother "for short of pegging his two lips together I can't think of anything!"

Aunt Mary glanced wickedly across to Uncle Ned where he was chuckling to himself and then she launched into a story which had caused a great deal of merriment at the table at Riley's that evening. It happened a short time previously on a warm evening when Uncle Ned had decided that as his milker was almost dry he would take his stool and can down and milk her in the field. He had grass to spare and had allowed the Riley's to graze a couple of young calves in the field. He settled himself and commenced when suddenly he got a violent puck in the back from one of the calves which upset the can. He shoo'd it off angrily and settled himself again only to get another shove in the back. He picked up the stool and made a swipe at the offending calf which was now joined by the other one and what with them pushing and shoving and trying to get their heads in the can he got no milk that evening. He picked up the can and set off for Riley's and told them, by now breathless with rage, to get those dratted calves out of the field before he did them an injury. Mrs Riley managed to calm him down by promising to do so and poured a suitable amount of milk into the can. All this had been watched by Pat and Mick, the culprits, from behind the hedge. The calves were hand reared and the lads used to call them by rattling the cans vigorously, so when they heard the rattle of Uncle Ned's can, naturally the calves thought it was feeding time.

There was lots to do that summer getting Uncle Ned settled in and, as he gradually got the new place fixed up, transferring Queenie, Spot and Cutie, to their new kennels which were sited well away from the bungalow. True to his word Uncle Ned got a pup, the intended watch-dog, a mongrel, of course, of indeterminate parentage, a fat little bundle of mischief with a thick curly coat of white mixed with black. Aunt Mary christened him at once, Bubbles.

Uncle Ned was outraged. He had often voiced his firm conviction that once a woman had anything to do with a dog he was thereafter useless for anything other than a pet.

"Bubbles" he said contemptuously. "Indade an' we won't call him any sich thing. Rex his name is. A foine name for a watch-dog Bubbles, I must say!"

But Bubbles it was, and Bubbles was no watch-dog. He was so friendly and welcoming to all and sundry that he would nearly fall over at the strength of his tail-wagging; and as he got older we realised that he would never do the job for which he was got, but Gran would not part with him for the world. As things turned out, however, we did not need him as such, for we got an unexpected and exceptionally competent stand-in.

As Uncle Ned's little bungalow was gradually fitted out for occupation it was decided that my mother, Jack, Hannah and I would move in until such time as my father found a home for us, with Gran continuing to occupy the old place in the village. All that winter we stayed there very happily and snugly until about April it was time for us to go to England to start our life there together. Gran was still loath to leave the village saying she would be too lonely, and she entreated my mother to leave me with her for the first few months until she got used to it. Uncle Ned and Aunt Mary added their pleas and so it was arranged.

Jack, of course, did not want to go either, but was somewhat mollified at the prospect of a ride to the station in a real car. Uncle Ned's pal, Paddy Dooley, had invested in a little car, the only one for miles around, with the intention of ferrying the local lads to the football matches and such like, hopefully earning a few shillings for himself thereby. We had already had a few little jaunts in it, to Jack's great delight, as he loved whizzing round the winding, twisting roads, and Paddy had promised to take him the longest and most winding way, or as Jack put it "We'll go by the curliest road, now, won't we, Paddy?"

"Indade we will Jack" said Paddy laughing "we'll go by the curliest road in the whole of the County Kildare."

So once more my mother set off on her journey "across the water" as she had done so many times before. She always stayed on deck as the atmosphere down below turned her stomach. I can remember how cold it was, no covered-in decks then, and we had to find as sheltered a spot as we could and huddle together wrapped in a rug for warmth. I was always a good sailor and did not mind how much we pitched and tossed — and pitched and tossed we were — the Irish Sea was often very rough. Luckily there were always plenty of porters willing to help with the children and carry the bags, finding seats for us on the train for a few pence.

We were lonely for a while after they left, of course, but we all had plenty to occupy us with the hustle and bustle of getting moved and settled in, and once Gran had her beloved "hins" installed in the secure stone-built little outhouse Uncle Ned had fixed up for them, she seemed quite happy.

Gran, in common with the other country women, was always trying to improve her stock of poultry, and would cadge a setting of eggs of a proven good laying breed from a neighbour, or exchange a young cockerel, or a broody hen, all with the hope of improving her strain. In this way she had come up with a pure bred Rhode Island Red cock, and as he grew to full maturity he was a splendid bird. He was the largest cock I have ever seen, a sight to behold with his gleaming bronzey feathers, bright red coxcomb and flowing tail feathers, strutting proudly round his little harem. He was also extremely bad-tempered, and, for some reason, he hated me. He hated all humans to be sure, even Gran got many a nasty peck if she dared to molest any of his wives, but I was his particular enemy. He would not let me out of the house, and on the rare occasions when I did venture out, he would commence a sort of prancing sideways dance in my direction, causing me to flee ignominiously, usually gaining the safety of the kitchen and slamming the half-door on his flailing talons only just in the nick of time.

No one could get either in or out with him on the prowl. The postman would not venture in under any circumstances, after one confrontation when he walked in all unsuspecting and had to beat a hasty retreat after using his mail bag, which luckily for him was rather heavy that day, to very good effect. Neighbours had to coo-ee to attract our attention from the gate, and Gran had to run after him armed with a sack to throw over him and lock him away in the hen house, and many a merry dance he led her, I can tell you, as he soon got wise to the purpose of the sack.

Eventually, of course, he became such a nuisance that Gran decided to get rid of him. This she did after she had a few clutches of chicks to continue the strain, as she said "Tis only full of sperrit he is, breedin'll always tell in the end!"

Mrs Riley was only too happy to take him, and, in return she gave Gran a setting of duck eggs, which Gran, immediately put under a good broody hen of her own, and I got a good deal of rather vindictive pleasure as I visualised the very rude awakening he was about to get when he tried his antics with Mrs Riley's half wild mongrels, none of which was a Bubbles, to run off yelping with his tail between his legs.

We had never had ducklings before and I waited impatiently for the day when they should make their appearance, and what adorable little yellow balls of fluff they were. There were eight of them, all fairly evenly matched except for one little thing which was very much smaller than the others, and which seemed to have the sight of only one eye.

Of course he became my especial little pet, and I took it upon myself to see that he at least got his fair share of grub as otherwise he would be pushed out by the other stronger ones. Uncle Ned fixed up a box, by joining two large tea-chests together, with a removable roof, to house them at night for the first few weeks so they would be cosy and safe. Early each morning I would bring out the first feed of the day and it was laughable to see the way they would all scatter as soon as the roof was lifted off, and my little one would usually make for a corner and would then find all the others had gone to other corners, and he would then start a frenzied skittering run round the box until he joined up with them, all the while trying to keep his one sound eye swivelled in my direction. Despite my care, though, sadly he only survived a couple of weeks.

The others all thrived, however, and as the days got warmer and they got stronger, Gran would let the mother hen and her little brood into the garden and she and I would sit on the garden seat chatting and watching them as they scurried busily hither and thither foraging for little titbits for themselves.

Sitting on the seat happily together one day my attention was diverted from the little ducklings as I watched a contest between two very unusual adversaries. "Oh, look at that, Gran" I said, and the two of us watched a sparring match between a little wren and a moth which was almost as large as he was himself. The two of them were hovering in the warm air, sizing one another up, and when one saw an opening it would dart in and the other would dodge out of the way. The moth was not in the least frightened of the wren, which amazed me as surely it should have been a most unequal contest, and, indeed was so bold as to make several attacking swoops which actually caused the little wren to back off. The two of them continued in this fashion for several minutes, feinting and weaving round one another without actually making contact until they got tired and both flew off in different directions.

I made a note of the direction in which the little wren had gone promising myself to see if I could find the nest. I had always had a great affection for the little birds, with their roly-poly look and up-tilted tail. I had often found an old nest and marvelled at the way it was designed, a complete ball of grass and moss with a tiny opening in the front, and I could imagine how snug the little ones would be in there protected from the wind and rain, and how tiny a newly-hatched nestling must be. I searched but did not find the nest. I never told anyone about any nests I found, apart from Uncle Ned and Gran, of course. They were my own secret, and I took great delight in inspecting each of my finds from time to time, never touching the eggs of course in case the mother would desert the nest. It was even more interesting when the eggs hatched and I could see how the nestlings were developing and how the slightest little rustle of the leaves caused the little beaks to open wide in anticipation. Mick Riley, who had a quite large collection of eggs, showed me a wren's egg once, the tiniest white egg with reddy brown speckles, and he said there were ten eggs in the nest he took it from, and it was intriguing to wonder how ten, sometimes even twelve, little birds could come to maturity in that little ball of a nest.

When I remonstrated with Mick for taking the eggs he replied hotly that he never took an egg unless there were several already in the nest and declared that he did not feel that the ones he took for his collection, one only of each species, would be missed. He said he felt as sad as me any time he found a nest that had been damaged and the eggs taken or broken, and, although in these circumstances we were rather too inclined to blame the village lads, we did not forget that there were several other hazards that the birds had to face, rats, magpies or crows, to mention but three. Mick had a great love for and took a great delight in the birds around and was a mine of information. He only had to get the merest glimpse or snatch of song to name the species, which I always found fascinating as I did not have much of an ear, or an eye for that matter, only being familiar with the most common ones.

One day when the ducklings were about three weeks old, we were sitting together on the bench not paying too much attention when the little mother hen started a loud alarmed squawking, and we looked up to see a large grey crow swooping down menacingly on the ducklings. Gran ran to get the broom and I ran to try to protect the ducklings, but it was an impossible task as, in their terror, they had scattered in all directions, and as Gran reappeared brandishing the broom, we saw the bird dive and get a little yellow body and carry it off swiftly. Gran and I set about collecting the others and had almost got them all together when the crow returned once more, and despite our efforts to beat him off, he snatched another and away again.

The memory of those feeble struggling little yellow bodies and the knowledge of their cruel fate upset me very much. Gran tried to comfort me by murmuring "Tis nature, agradh. Ye can't change that" but she was upset too, but for a different reason, her clutch of ducklings was now reduced to five. These five thrived during the coming months, and, luckily, all five were ducks so there were duck eggs now for the table, not that I ever liked them, too strong for my taste, but Gran and Uncle Ned were partial to a nice duck egg for tea.

After a few weeks, Gran decided to get a drake for the ducks so that she could sell a few clutches of fertile eggs and Mrs Riley came up trumps again. She had a somewhat elderly drake of the same breed, they were all pure white, that she did not want any longer. He was a large drake and in tiptop condition except for the fact that he had a large lump of some kind right in the middle of one of his webbed feet, which made his naturally ungraceful gait positively ludicrous as he took his rightful place at the head of his wives and tried as well as he could to negotiate the very pebbly yard. Once into the fields he fared better on the soft grass.

All went well until one evening as Gran and I were shepherding them into their house for the night, a light aeroplane suddenly appeared and flew low over us with engines roaring. Where it came from no one knew, perhaps it was a military training flight, but it was a most unusual occurrence, and the effect on the ducks was startling. They immediately started a pell-mell rush for their house, trampling their lord and master well and truly in the process. First one, then all the others in quick succession, trampled over him flattening him in the mud, and each time he struggled to his feet another knocked him flat again, tumbling head over heels over one another in their haste. Finally he managed to pick himself up, cocked an enraged eye at Gran and me where we were doubled up with laughter, shook his ruffled feathers and waddled off with as much dignity as he could muster.

"Oh Lord bless us and save us" said Gran wiping her eyes "what in the world got inta thim? They must've thought it was the auld crow coming for thim agin!"

Our Pet Robin

One afternoon as I was very happily helping Uncle Ned to prepare the pups' grub, I saw a little robin cheekily hopping round his feet picking up any crumbs as they fell. I caught Uncle Ned's eye and silently pointed and he put his fingers up to his lips and carried on with what he was doing, ostensibly taking no notice but at the same time throwing little scraps his way. He seemed quite unafraid of Uncle Ned but kept a very wary eye out for me, and when he had enough he flew off.

Uncle Ned told me he had been putting in an appearance any time food was on the go for some time, gradually getting tamer and tamer until he was actually alighting on the rim of the pot in which he was mixing the food. Soon Uncle Ned only had to walk out into the yard for our little pet to join him, swooping down from a nearby perch where he had been waiting, and he would hop about after him watching everything with his bright inquisitive eyes.

Then he started to follow Uncle Ned to the kitchen and wait outside the door for him to reappear, until one blowy day Uncle Ned closed the door behind him and he flew onto the sill of the kitchen window where he hopped about eyeing us through the glass.

The next step was to appear on the ledge of the open window and there he would perch watching until one morning when Uncle Ned was having his breakfast and had cut the rinds off his bacon and put them on the edge of his plate, he swooped down, lifted one of the rinds and was away again out the window trailing his prize behind him.

He was soon coming and going at will and would hop all over the cottage and several times he gave me a fright when I came upon him unexpectedly and I would flee screaming thinking he was a mouse for the moment, as we always got a few especially round about harvest time, and I dreaded them. Needless to say we all took a great delight in our little visitor as we awaited with interest the next step in our relationship.

Then one very busy day as Gran and I were preparing to set about the weekly churning of the delicious country butter which I loved, he blotted his copy-book by dropping a little calling card right in the bowl of the separator into which Gran was pouring the milk.

"Bad scran to ye annyway" said Gran and shooed him out forthwith and closed the window. "That'll fix ye for a while" she said as she poured away the milk into Queenie's dish and thoroughly washed out the bowl before starting afresh. All the while we were making the butter he would alight on the sill, eye us very crossly, than eye the closed window equally as crossly, and fly off in disgust. We were both unable to stop laughing at his antics "Bedad, an' that's no robin" said Gran "it's a fairy, it's been bewitched!"

When Uncle Ned came in he was very amused also at our little pet's performance, and after watching for a few moments he turned to me and said "We'll have to look out for Queenie, Jen. She'll have him if she gets half a chance as ye well know. He's getting a bit too cheeky. He'll take one chance too many if he doesn't watch out and that 'ud be a turrible pity, wouldn't it now?"

I knew to what Uncle Ned was referring. Every year swallows nested in the old outhouses in the yard and we were delighted to see them return time after time, but once as a mother swallow was returning to her little ones to feed them she had flown too near to Queenie, who with a lightning snap had caught her by the tail. Uncle Ned immediately managed to make Queenie release her but her tail was badly damaged, half of the long fork being torn away. She rejoined her fellows and they swooped and dived all round her with loud cries of alarm. We could see her clearly in amongst them, her damaged tail making her stand out from the others. Uncle Ned put Queenie into her paddock and we waited anxiously to see if the swallow would return to her hungry little ones, but she never did, so Uncle Ned brought the nest into the kitchen with three little nestlings in it, fairly well advanced so that we were hopeful that we would be able to rear them, but, despite the fact that we did our best to catch flies and insects, their natural food, sadly none survived. It was that incident that Uncle Ned had particularly in mind when he warned me to keep a watchful eye on Queenie whilst she was loose in the yard.

All that winter our little pet continued to favour us with his visits and as the weather got more severe he would perch on the fender in front of the range revelling in the warmth as he twisted and turned in his efforts to dry off his cold wet feathers.

One particularly cold sleety morning old Mickey Flood called to deliver some bread for Uncle Ned. Mickey kept a few pigs and used to collect any stale unsold bread from the local small town bakeries and would give Uncle Ned a few loaves for Queenie and the pups.

Gran took pity on Mickey who was blue with the cold and asked him in to warm himself and soon had a plate of bacon and eggs, her delicious home-made wheaten bread and a scalding hot cup of tea set before him, and Mickey tucked in heartily. He soon had his plate cleared and was just settling back for a few puffs on his pipe when our little pet swooshed past his ear, took the rind and was away again so swiftly that Mickey nearly fell backwards off the chair he was so startled.

"What in hiven's name was that?" he said and on Gran telling him the tale he was highly amused.

"He must've mistook ye for Ned" said Gran "ye're sittin' in his place!"

Soon our little pet appeared on his usual perch in the open window and sat there for a few minutes surveying us warily, but deciding all was well, down he flew again on to the fender and set about drying his feathers once more, opening his wings to the warmth and turning and twisting until he was quite satisfied before flying off again. Mickey was entranced.

"Well niver in all me life have I heerd or seen the like av that" he said. "I saw Fr Rafferty on his rounds down the road apiece. He'd love to be presinted to that little craytur I've no doubt atall."

Mickey grinned at us and we grinned back at him. We knew

what he meant. As I said Mickey kept a few pigs and once when he had a particularly good yardful and Fr Rafferty had been visiting, in his anxiety to show them off he had rushed up to him, caught him by the arm and cried "Ah, ye can't go yet, Father, not before I show ye to me pigs."

Fr Rafferty, being a farmer's son himself, was quite willing to "be shown" to the pigs, laughing heartily at the same time, and every time he had met Mickey since he had asked about the pigs.

Sure enough, Fr Rafferty soon put in an appearance at the kitchen door, and settled himself down to enjoy a cup of tea with us after asking Mickey the familiar question "Any dacent pigs this time Mickey?" and receiving the reply "None worth yer attintion, yer Riverence, nary a one!"

Father Rafferty was a great bit of a sport. He loved to hunt whenever he could and he kept a couple of coursing dogs himself and, naturally took a lively interest in Uncle Ned's pups also. He had taken a great liking to Jack whom he termed "a grand little lad" ever since their first meeting. Jack was almost two at the time and had come to the conclusion that every male visitor to the house was called Paddy and he greeted all and sundry with a cheerful "Hallo Paddy".

When Father Rafferty had called Jack met him at the door with the usual "Hallo Paddy".

"Jack" said Gran warningly, but Father Rafferty had laughed and said "Shure, an isn't the child right? Am I not a Paddy?"

Mickey soon launched into the tale of the robin, and Father Rafferty sat with us for quite a while hoping that our little pet would put in an appearance, but he did not. I suppose two visitors and all the unusual talk and bustle kept him away, but we were all very disappointed.

It was in the spring that we became aware for the first time that our pet was a she and not a he, there being no difference between the cock and hen robin as regards appearance, as one day as he was picking up little titbits for himself from the kitchen floor there suddenly appeared a second robin, which perched very nervously on the ledge and there ensued between the two what sounded suspiciously like a domestic row with the new robin calling very insistently and crossly, and our little pet replying coolly and just carrying on very offhandedly with what she was doing. The second robin flew off only to reappear a few minutes later to repeat the performance. This time our robin followed him swiftly when he flew off.

After that he would follow her every time she came in to the kitchen, always perching on the ledge and calling until she flew after him. I knew that they would be building a nest and raising a family, and I searched the hedgerows and all the most likely places, such as old kettles and pots and holes in walls, and I tried to watch where they went, but I never found the nest. In the days that followed the second robin would sometimes also come in to the kitchen but always very nervously and would stay only a few moments and then away swiftly again.

This went on for a few more weeks and then the second robin stopped coming and we were left with our little friend to ourselves once again.

Then sometime towards the winter she too stopped coming and we never saw her again. We were all anxious about her and missed her a great deal. The weather that year was particularly severe and Uncle Ned warned us several times about a large rat he had seen prowling near the larder window. He inspected the window carefully especially the upper section, which consisted of strong metal with tiny holes in it which allowed air to circulate, to satisfy himself that the rat could not gain entry.

A few evenings later, on a very frosty night whilst we were all gathered together in the cosy kitchen, we heard a scratching sound at the window. Gran picked up the oil lamp, pulled the curtains and looked out to see what had caused the sound, and there on the sill we saw the large rat with a small brown bird which he held fast in his jaws by the neck, and the sound we had heard was the frantic, despairing, scratching of the little creature's claws.

I turned to Gran "Oh, Gran, can't we do something?"

"No, agradh" she said "it's too late" and indeed it was, already I could see the struggles weakening and the eyes beginning to glaze. Gran let the curtains close on the horrible evil head and wicked beady eyes, the owner of which had made no attempt to move when we shone the light on it, just sat there at its sickening work.

Feeling sad and upset I suddenly had a most horrifying

thought. I jumped up crying "Oh, Gran, it couldn't have been our little robin could it?"

"I don't think so, agradh" said Gran. "It was a little brown bird right enough but it didn't look like a robin to me."

"But our robin would very likely choose to roost in the rose-bush under the kitchen window, wouldn't she Gran?" I asked.

"Aye, very likely she would" said Gran "but don't forget we haven't seen her for a while now, and, annyway, I don't think it was a robin, it had no red breast that I could see!"

I sat miserably wondering what had happened to our little pet. Robins are territorial and will quite viciously see off another robin if it dares to intrude so I knew it more than likely that something had happened, especially as we had provided such easy pickings for her.

It was a few weeks after that unpleasant incident that Uncle Ned came to the kitchen and called me.

"Come out here, Jen. I have somethin' to show ye!"

"What is it?" I said.

"Come out now and ye'll see" he said.

I followed him out to the yard where he set about crumbling up bread for Queenie. I watched quietly for a few minutes and then I saw it, a young, sleek robin picking up the little crumbs about Uncle Ned's feet, and then alighting on the edge of the pot as he moved away a little. It must be one of her nestlings, I thought, it must, come to take over the old homestead, and I rushed in happily to tell Gran.

A Great Delicacy

One beautiful June morning I awoke early and became aware of a scratching noise outside my window. I jumped out of bed, pulled the curtains and looked out to see if I could find out what it was. I could see no reason for the noise, so I went back to bed as it was quite early and no one was yet astir. I lay in bed wondering what the noise was that had awakened me, when the sound started up again, and this time I realised what it was.

One day a short time previously Uncle Ned had left a small can that he sometimes used to carry a drink of fresh water out to the yard for the dogs on the window-sill of my bedroom after using the contents, intending to pick it up later on his way to the kitchen, and had forgotten to do so. It had remained on the sill for a few days until he remembered it, but when he went to get it, he discovered that a little blue tit had started to build her nest in the can.

He decided to leave her to her task and came to the kitchen to tell Gran and me about it. It was one of those cans, usually used for carrying paraffin oil but, of course, had never been used for that purpose. I was intrigued.

"What a funny place for her to choose!" I said to Uncle Ned.

"Well, they do choose all sorts of odd places like that!" he said.

"But how will the little ones get out of the can?" I asked.

"Ah, whin the time comes they'll get out, that ye can be shure av" said Uncle Ned.

The time had arrived that morning as the noise which had awakened me was the little blue tits leaving the nest and having quite a bit of difficulty doing so as well. I could visualise the six or seven little things there in the dark with only that very small opening six or so inches above them to aim for in their bid for freedom.

One by one the little birds appeared, after much scratching on the sides of the can, balanced themselves on the rim for a few seconds to take in this bright, new, frightening world opening up before them, and then joined their mother in a nearby bush where she had stationed herself, loudly encouraging her offspring to come to her. The last one of all seemed to have the most difficulty, as it took some time to accomplish the feat and seemed almost exhausted when it did eventually put in an appearance, but after a little rest it, too, managed to fly off to the bush.

As soon as I heard someone stirring I got up and went to the kitchen to tell Gran and Uncle Ned all about it.

"I hope that last little one will be all right" I said.

"I hope so too" said Uncle Ned. "If I'd known about it I could've turned the can on its side to make it aisier for thim!"

"Oh, I wish I had thought of that" I said.

"Ye see Jen" said Uncle Ned "that last little one was probably the youngest and weakest of the brood. Also the mother coaxes and encourages thim, little by little, from one branch to the next, until they gradually get stronger and can fly further. Now if that little one was too far behind the others he could be quite unable to keep up and would have no chance!"

I looked miserable.

"Well let's go and see if we can spot thim. They can't have gone too far yet" he said.

We searched the garden and the adjoining hedges, but no sign did we find of the little blue tit or her family.

The days of that summer were passing happily but all too quickly, the last one I was to spend with Gran. It had been decided that I would stay for another year as my parents were unable to come over on holiday, the expense and difficulty of settling in a new home had been more than they had expected.

Aunt Mary was working in Dublin and only came down at weekends. Uncle Ned took an occasional day off to visit her and it was after one of these jaunts to the Capital that he produced a small jar and presented it to Gran.

"There ye are Mam a little present for ye" he said.

"What is it, Ned?" asked Gran.

"Wait yet now an' ye'll see" he said.

We all gathered round as he opened the jar and emptied the contents onto a plate and we all stood speechless eyeing the black mess on the plate.

"What in Hiven's name is it?" asked Gran at last.

"It's called caviare, some special fish's eggs" said Uncle Ned. "It's considered a great delicacy and much sought after by the gintry!"

"D'ye mane to tell me that the gintry ate that?" asked Gran.

"Indade they do" said Uncle Ned "they go mad for it!"

"Ah, go on with ye, Ned" laughed Gran. "I don't believe a word of it!"

"Tis true as I stand here" said Uncle Ned. "D'ye know that if ye were in England now ye'd have to ask the King's permission before ye could take a mouthful."

"Arrah, go on with ye" said Gran and she laughed again.

"Ye're supposed to ate it on toast" said Uncle Ned. "Ye can do the toast Jen" and when I did he cut it in four, spreading some of the caviare on each piece.

He offered it to Gran. "Begorrah, an' I wouldn't ate that if I was starvin' " she said. "Nor me nayther" said Aunt Mary.

"Ye'll try a bit, Jen, won't ye?" said Uncle Ned to me. I took a piece and bit into it reluctantly, immediately rushing to the kitchen door to spit it out.

"It's awful!" I said.

Uncle Ned tried his bit, managing to swallow a mouthful.

"Well I have to agree with ye there" he said.

"What'll we do with it?" he asked.

"Give it to auld Minchie" said Aunt Mary. "She'll ate it all right!"

Minchie was an old half-wild Manx cat that had turned up at the kitchen door one day and she would indeed eat anything. She was a great ratter and mouser but she also got many a baby rabbit or bird which made me chase her off. So the great and much sought after delicacy was put before Minchie who took one sniff and fled not to be seen again for three days.

I do not think that Minchie was a true Manx cat. She probably lost her tail through an accident, perhaps in a trap. One day she appeared in the backyard with two very scrawny tabby kittens both with long elegant tails. It was the only time she ever brought any of her offspring home, whether that was because they were the only ones she ever had or because some danger threatened them particularly, we did not know, but we soon fattened them up and they became very affectionate, a thing their mother never did. She was always wary and unapproachable. One beautiful sunny day Gran and I were out in the backyard weeding and generally tidying up or "scuffling" as Gran called it, and the two kittens were playing happily together with Minchie looking on indulgently from the roof of the hen house. Gran had made a large currant soda cake which she was baking in the pot oven, a large cast iron pot standing on three legs, which she had placed in a makeshift fireplace made of large stones, piling glowing turf underneath and all round the sides and on the lid.

She often baked her bread this way on very hot days when the range would not be lit and the cakes cooked slowly and beautifully inside the pot. When it was cooked Gran removed the oven and placed the large black kettle on the embers for the tea. Suddenly Minchie sprang down from the hen house, picked up one of her kittens, which rolled itself into a little ball so that she could carry it more easily, leapt through the open glass doors and deposited the kitten in the scullery and came back for the other one. We were both very surprised because Minchie had never ventured into the cottage before. Gran told me to bring the kittens back out into the sunlight, but as fast as I did Minchie grabbed them up and back inside with them again.

"What's got inta the craytur?" said Gran. At that moment there was a violent hailstorm and soon the little concreted square was covered with large hailstones and the hissing and smoking fire was soon out. We looked at one another. Minchie had known that hailstorm was coming several minutes before, which was more than we did despite the fact that Gran always prided herself on being a very good judge of the weather.

Gran had great patience but she was also reputed to have a terrible temper when provoked, but I only ever saw one instance of Gran in a rage and it happened one day whilst we were all pottering in the kitchen and Gran, hearing the squeak of the gate, looked out the window peering to see who it was. Suddenly with a loud cry she grabbed up the broom, opened the door and ran out. My mother, Aunt Mary, and I followed hastily, not knowing what to expect, and we were in time to see Gran, clutching the broom, advancing quickly towards the gate where old Farmer Brogan was leading Jack towards us rather roughly by the ear. We did not hear what she said but we did see her raise the broom very threateningly and certainly Farmer Brogan departed rather more quickly than he came in.

She put her arm round Jack comfortingly as they walked back together to the kitchen door. Uncle Ned put in an appearance and asked "What was that all about Mam?"

"Ah, 'twas that auld Brogan" said Gran "said Jack knocked the haystacks down jumpin' on thim. 'Twas the way he brought him in though I minded. Look what he's done to the child's ear" she said, still furious, as she showed Jack's red, swollen ear and tearful face.

As Uncle Ned looked he got as angry as Gran. "I've a good mind to go down and have it out with him" he said.

"Oh, no, Ned don't do that" said my mother anxious to avoid further trouble. "Jack shouldn't have been jumping on the stacks."

"Ah, shure, every kid in the place was there doin' the same I've no doubt" said Uncle Ned "but he caught Jack naturally. He isn't as cute as the others. An' I can tell ye he wouldn't've led anny other kid home by the ear, he'd have got a stick over the head!"

"An' that's what I should've done" said Gran. "I should've hit him over the head with the broom!"

"I thought ye were goin' to once or twice" said Aunt Mary.

"Ah I mind him well since me young day" said Gran. "He was niver much good, as cross as a bag av cats always, with a look on his face that's enough to turn milk sour!"

"An' the manest man to walk this earth to boot" said Aunt Mary who had firsthand experience as she helped out sometimes at the farm during busy times. "He's that mane he wouldn't give ye the skin av a nut for nothin'!"

"Aye" said Gran "he hates partin' wi' money as much as the

E

divil hates holy water!"

"I'll niver forget the time he put that auld lump of fat before the lads" said Aunt Mary. "That took a hard neck to do I'm tellin' ye! The toughest, fattest auld pig he ever killed!" and she launched for the umpteenth time into the tale of how one day when she was helping out at the farm during haymaking she had been ashamed to set the horrible, greasy, quivering slab of bacon before the local lads who were lending a neighbourly hand to gather in the hay, and how Paddy Dooley, cupping his chin in his hands, and gazing reflectively at the repulsive lump for a minute or two, had remarked gently "Ah, ye can stop shiverin' for faith I have no intintion whatsomniver of touching ye!"

"An' what's it all for" said Gran "an' him with nayther chick nor child to lave it all to!"

"To be the richest man in the graveyard" said Aunt Mary "that's what it's for!"

"Well that he'll surely be" said Gran. "It must be awful hard for the like av him to have to lave it all behind!"

"It must indade" said Aunt Mary.

"Well annyway I told him a thing or two about himself that he won't forget in a hurry" said Gran with great satisfaction.

A Contrairy Auld Yoke

I loved the long summer days but I enjoyed the long winter evenings too, when the evening meal was over, and we had said the Rosary together, Gran and I would settle ourselves on one side of the glowing peat fire, with Grandad on the other, contentedly puffing on his pipe and listening as I read out loud from one of the little books of stories that Uncle Ned used to buy me any time he went to town. Lovely stories they were, of fairies and witches, princes and princesses, Greek heroes facing and overcoming every hazard in their eternal wanderings round the isthmus and islands of far away and romantic lands. I loved that word "isthmus" although, of course, I had no idea whatever of what it meant.

Gran enjoyed those stories as much as I did. Her favourite one was that of the princess who was so delicate and genteel that she could feel a pea if she lay on it even through several mattresses. She loved the picture papers that my mother sent over regularly and would eagerly scan the pages for pictures of royalty and "the gintry".

She was incurably romantic, simple in her ways but by no means stupid. Both she and my Grandfather came from the West of Ireland; but whilst my Grandfather had travelled, having been in the British Army; Gran had never been out of Ireland and vowed that nothing would ever induce her to leave it.

My very earliest memory of Gran was of holding her hand

tightly as we set out on a little walk together. I had on a new pair of white kid boots, and I remember sitting on Gran's knee as she did up all the side buttons with a little hook. How delighted and proud I was walking with Gran with my new boots.

Gran had on her most prized possession too, a beautiful black curly haired fur coat that she called "me carracool". It came right down to her ankles and on top of her head she wore a black velour hat firmly skewered by several large hat pins. It was years later that I found out that "carracool" was Gran's Gaelicised version of the proper name for the fur, and I have often wondered just how Gran ever became possessed of such a beautiful and exotic thing as a real Persian lamb coat.

I don't remember what she looked like at that time, but from all accounts I have had she was considered a very good-looking woman. I do remember that she was tall and slim, which she remained always, and, in fact, she had a great aversion to fat on anyone, and especially on any of her own family. Her hair was beautiful, golden brown, thick and glossy, and when she let it down it reached beyond her waist. Her most striking feature, however, were her eyes, a lovely clear gray colour, an asset she did not pass on to any of her family who were all blue-eyed like my Grandfather.

My Grandfather too was considered a fine figure of a man although not much above average height he was very strong, fair skinned and blue-eyed, with a luxuriant moustache waxed at the ends.

When we had no book to read I would encourage Gran to tell me of "her young day" as she called it, not that she needed much encouragement, she enjoyed talking about her life as much as I enjoyed listening to her. She was the youngest of her family and stayed with her mother when she became widowed, the rest of the family all emigrated to America and all contact with them was lost over the years. Her mother, somehow or other, provided a living for the two of them by means of a little fruit and vegetable stall which she ran at the local market place. Gran told me that her mother's two great pleasures in life were her old clay pipe and the hot strong tea which she kept constantly on the brew on the hob. Once when she was feeling unwell the local doctor warned her that she had to give up both of them at once. She gave up neither and great was her glee when she survived him by a good thirty years.

She was 102 when she died and every soul for miles round turned up at her funeral to pay their last respects. It was the event of the decade.

Gran married young and would have had thirteen children if all had gone right, but she had several miscarriages and in the end there were six children, one, a girl, died at about three or four, and they lost their eldest boy, a fine athletic lad of fifteen when he fell from the high bars in the gym one day, got meningitis and never recovered. This was a very hard blow to them indeed.

Grandfather was a great walker and would go for miles round the country roads with Jackie as companion. When Jackie died, my mother, who also always thoroughly enjoyed a good walk, took his place, and she told me once of how Grandfather would weep bitterly to himself for long afterwards, and the effect this had on her to see him, big and strong as he was. They would not return home until he had recovered himself and could act normally again.

Gran had a great sense of humour, was as lively as a bee, interested in everything going on in the world. On looking back now I am amazed at how well educated they were considering they both came from such a remote and wild part of the country, and this was well over a hundred years ago. Both could read and write extremely well and could do their sums quite competently. She could play the accordion very well, self-taught and only for family amusement, "vamping" she called it. It took very little to make Gran happy, as she often said to me "If ye're continted, agradh, ye have everythin' in life."

She was intensely interested in my other Grandmother. The two old ladies never met and lived completely different lives, but there were also many things in common. Gran lived all her life in the country, Grandma was born and never moved away from the bustling Midlands of England. Both of them had a lively humorous outlook on life and both had to work hard to bring up their families, and by a curious coincidence Grandma also had thirteen children, six surviving, but her losses were sustained by losing both or one of several sets of twins. Gran was tall, Grandma was the tiniest, neatest little woman I have ever known. I never saw Gran in anything but dark skirts down to her ankles, and she must have been a young woman, in her early forties, when I first took note. Grandma kept abreast of the fashions as best she could, had her hair permed right up until the end, and I particularly remember Gran's amazement when I told her that Grandma had only just had her own teeth removed and had false teeth for the first time at the age of seventy.

As we passed the evenings so happily, the days were passing very quickly also. Uncle Ned had bought a donkey and cart to fetch and carry. All the water had to be brought from the nearest pump, and often in the winter the pumps would freeze up and that meant a trek until you found one that was working and that was quite a chore. Uncle Ned could now get several good sized cans in one go. He could also go to the Bog of Allen for a load of turf whenever he wanted. The donkey, of course, true to its breed was unpredictable and stubborn, and if it took a mind to it would stick its four legs to the road and nothing would budge it. The only person who could handle it was Gran. The two of them developed some sort of understanding with one another, so much so that Gran only had to put in an appearance at the kitchen door for the donkey to lift its head and give out a loud hee-haw.

One afternoon when Uncle Ned had been on a trip to the Bog and had been away nearly all day, Gran was beginning to be worried when he put in an appearance, breathless with rage, saying the old donkey had been even more stubborn than usual and was at that moment a short distance from home, refusing to move, and would Gran come and see if she could do anything.

Gran set off with Uncle Ned and I went and opened the gates in readiness. As soon as the donkey saw Gran he took off towards her and as Gran realised he had no intention of stopping she somehow or other grabbed hold of his mane hanging on for dear life, and, in true Western fashion, managed to turn him in at the gate notwithstanding the danger to life and limb.

Uncle Ned came running up and was relieved to see both

Gran and the donkey perfectly all right, and as he and I went back to collect the sods of turf which had fallen off the cart all along the road during the donkey's gallop, I started to laugh as I remembered how Gran had looked as the donkey pulled her along, her feet only barely touching the ground now and again, showing more slender black stockinged leg than she ever had in her life, all the hairpins jogged out of her bun and her hair flying round her, shouting "Whoa there, can't ye! Whoa, ye contrairy auld yoke! Whoa whin I tell ye!"

When we got back Uncle Ned asked Gran how on earth she had managed to grab hold of the donkey's head that way. "Well now I don't know rightly how I did it" said Gran "it seems there's a spark or two av life left in me yet I didn't even know I had meself!" and she laughed.

It was on another of those trips to the Bog when Uncle Ned had taken me along and we were on our way home that I espied a little hedgehog slowly crossing the road and in imminent danger of being run down by the cart. Uncle Ned jumped down and picked the little creature up and brought it back for me to see. It was only a young one and did not seem to be afraid of us and we examined it closely for a few minutes, noting the sharp spines, the little feet with their five strong claws, the rather prominent but poor-sighted eyes. Hedgehogs are nocturnal and it was uncommon to see one in daylight.

"We'll take it home to show Mam" said Uncle Ned and he put it in his cap where it lay seemingly content. When we arrived back Uncle Ned called Gran and when she came he put the cap with the little creature in it in her hands. "Arrah, Ned" cried Gran "what d'ye mane by putting it in yer cap? Don't ye know that they're full av fleas?"

"Are they now, Mam?" said Uncle Ned as he put it down at our feet.

"Alive with thim" said Gran crossly.

We stood looking as it stayed motionless where Uncle Ned had put it.

"Give him a sup av milk" said Uncle Ned.

"Yes," said Gran "bring one av Minchie's saucers, not one av my good ones!"

Gran was very fastidious and had nearly had a fit once when she was having a cup of tea in a neighbour's and the hostess had put down a few titbits for the cat and then calmly picked up the plate and put it back on the table.

The little creature thirstily lapped the milk. "He likes that" said Uncle Ned.

"Oh, aye" said Gran "they like milk right enough. They'll suckle cows in the field if they get half a chance an all!"

"Who told ye that tale?" said Uncle Ned disparagingly.

"Oh, 'tis true enough" said Gran "I always heerd tell av it!"

"We'll put him in the garden" said Uncle Ned "he'll clear it av slugs in no time."

He put it on the path leading to the garden and it made its way slowly towards the cabbage patch.

Gran laughed "It's just like an old man" she said.

And that is exactly what it did look like as it ambled along, stopping to turn round to look at us when we all laughed, before disappearing from view.

Whenever the circus came Uncle Ned would always take me and we would always go on the hobby horses, my favourite ride, as many times as we had the money for, and once, when I was younger he had taken me to see a production of 'The Wedding of the Painted Doll' which was staged by a travelling players' company. I was thrilled, I thought it simply wonderful, and as we rode home, with me sitting on the crossbar of Uncle Ned's bike, the two of us sang the theme song all along the country roads.

Then if there was a suitable film on he would take me and I will never ever forget the day we went to see 'King Kong'. It was a sensation and just about everyone for miles around tried to get into the little local tin-roofed cinema to see it, with the result that we were packed in like sardines, and as it was a blistering hot afternoon it was literally an oven inside. Everytime the reel broke down, which was often, the doors were thrown open and everyone stampeded for the daylight and gasped in the beautiful fresh air.

On these occasions Gran would always get us an extra little treat for tea, and I would wonder all the way home what it would be, my gastric juices beginning to flow in anticipation. Would it be her lovely dark fruit cake, her apple or rhubarb tart with its melt in the mouth pastry, or a farrel of potato cake, hot and thickly buttered. As we tucked in Gran would listen as we described what we had seen down to the merest detail. Gran had only ever been to the pictures once in her life and Aunt Mary had told me about it. When the family were growing up they had lived in the large army camp, this was in the British time of course, where Grandfather had a job in the Ordinance Dept. They had a comfortable house with a spare bedroom and, to provide a little extra income, Gran used to take in "turns" who were performing at the picture house. So they always got free tickets and on this occasion, my mother and Aunt Mary had persuaded her to accompany them. As luck would have it, it was one of those disaster movies with a horrific train crash, and Gran got completely absorbed, so much so that when they showed the inevitable shot of the train seemingly coming straight down on them, she forgot where she was and started to scream hysterically. The film was stopped, the lights put on, and my mother and Aunt Mary had to take her out of the picture house, with everyone craning to get a better look. They were both furious, of course, as Aunt Mary said "She made a holy show of us"; and that was the one and only time that Gran saw a picture show.

I remember that house on the camp also very well. It was from there that Gran and I set out on the walk we took together. I remember the snowy cotton counterpane on the bed, and Gran tucking me in after we had said the prayers together and how she would go round the room flicking the holy water which she kept in a little bottle with a feather in it to sprinkle it round.

If it was a wild night Gran would always pause and say "Listen to that wind!" and, no doubt remembering the many tragedies amongst the fisherfolk plying their trade in their flimsy boats on that wild rocky coast in her youth, would add the prayer "God bless and protect anyone at sea this night." Sometimes she would croon old Irish lullabys before I snuggled down in my warm bed with the light of the little red Sacred Heart lamp serving the dual purpose also of night-light, and the picture of my Guardian Angel gazing down on me where lying on my side I could see it quite clearly and feeling secure and protected under his care.

It was in that house that my mother grew up very comfortably. In addition to my Grandfather having a steady job and the little extra brought in by Gran's lodgers, any woman who was handy with the needle could pick up extra money by literally "sewing shirts for soldiers". The shirts would be cut out and delivered in batches ready for sewing, and they received the sum of 9d. for each one which passed the rather strict inspection, and that would be a very handy little income indeed, for 9d. was very good money in those days. As the girls came of age they also got jobs in the Ordinance, also making shirts and other garments for the soldiers, and I was staggered when my mother told me that she received the quite princely sum of £1 a week, and this would be around about the time of the end of the First World War. It was more than her father was earning, and certainly more than the soldiers themselves were getting. When I commenced work as a shorthand typist I received twenty-five shillings a week, so that will give you some idea of why I was staggered. In addition in the evening the girls had a certain number of shirts to do also to help Gran do her allotted batch. So all in all they were very comfortably off financially. It was from there, also, that my Aunt Jane and my mother married and left home to live in barracks and eventually moved off when the Free State took over. Grandfather had an opportunity to move to Britain also at the time but he stayed in Ireland, as Gran would not leave, and he was lucky enough to be kept on in his job by the incoming Irish Authorities. The crunch came, as they knew it would, when Grandfather retired and they had to leave the house also, and it was then that they moved to the village.

As I said before, Gran was an incurable romantic and one of my favourite tales was the story of how my Aunt Jane met her true love. I wrote it out once in the form of a short story and this I set out below.

Jane and the Dashing Lancer

Jane stood in front of the full length mirror surveying herself critically. What she saw was a slim girl of almost eighteen, not really pretty but attractive with her small regular features, clear pale skin, too pale she thought to herself, and the mass of dark hair piled up on her small head, tiny wavy tendrils of which framed her face.

It was her dress, however, that was occupying her attention at that moment. She had made it herself under the watchful eye of Mrs Fogarty, the local dressmaker, to whom she was apprenticed, especially for the big dance tonight, the last one of the season, the high spot of the winter. Also it was to be given by the Lancers, the most glamorous regiment on the army camp at that time, and invitations to their dances were much sought after and highly prized.

Jane was looking forward to it immensely. She could see it all now in her mind's eye as she twirled and twisted, this way and that, in front of the mirror. The men in their dress uniform, spotless white gloves, and the black patent leather dancing shoes without which no one was allowed on the floor. Oh, it would be marvellous, thought Jane, but would the dress do and would he be there? She did not want to appear countryish amidst the other girls who would be dressed up to the nines on this night of all nights, and, perhaps, horror of horrors, be a wallflower for the evening, especially with her mother, Mrs Fitzroy, sitting up in the gallery watching all that was going on and, with two other daughters coming up to marriageable age, very anxious that Jane should make a good match.

She thought once again of the way she had got the precious invitation. How she had been walking home from Mrs Fogarty's one afternoon and was well aware of the admiring glances of a group of young Lancers standing laughing and joking together, and how, just as she was passing, one of them asked, very politely, if he could have a word with her. She hesitated, but reassured by his appearance and manner, stopped, whereupon the young man told her of the forthcoming dance and asked if she would like an invitation. Jane was embarrassed by the several pairs of masculine eyes surveying her, but managed to say that she would very much like an invitation, she had never had one before. The young man replied that if she would tell him her name and address, he would see that she was put on the invitation list.

Jane rushed home full of the incident to tell her mother all about it, and when the gilt-edged invitation duly arrived requesting the pleasure of the company of Miss Jane Fitzroy at the dance, it was hard to know who was the more pleased Jane or her mother. Mrs Fitzroy had a great admiration for the Lancers, they were so smart and dashing, and had a particular interest in a young sergeant whom she had often seen around the camp walking or riding but most often escorting the Matron of the Army Hospital on her daily early morning rides. She had often spoken of him wondering who he was.

Since the invitation had arrived, Jane and her mother had been engaged in a happy flurry of activity. They had made several trips into the nearest small townships in their search for suitable materials, and after much discussion had finally settled on a deep rose pink georgette which Jane had made up into a full-skirted, tight bodiced dress which accentuated her tiny waist, and the colour suited her, it seemed to throw a reflected rosy tint onto her pale skin, and now here she was in her new dress, bathed, her hair brushed until it gleamed, ready to sally forth to see what the evening would bring.

Mrs Fitzroy bustled in at this moment, ready dressed to accompany Jane to the dance. No well-brought up young lady was allowed to go unchaperoned in those days, and woe betide Jane if she did not conduct herself in the manner in which Mrs Fitzroy thought a young lady should. She surveyed her daughter with pride and affection, "Yes, Jane, I think you'll do" she said. "Here, wear this for the evening" and she put her one much valued piece of jewellery, a golden pendant encrusted with garnets, round Jane's neck. "That will just put the finishing touch. Now put your coat on and we'll be off."

She went out of the room, but Jane was still not satisfied with her looks. She gave her nose a light dusting of powder, the only permitted aid to beauty, but, thinking again she was too pale, she resorted to a strategem she had often employed, and of which her mother was in complete ignorance, to solve the problem. She lightly rubbed her fingers over the red cloth book cover binding which was common at the time, transferring the resultant light stain to her cheeks, then a final faint dusting of powder.

On arrival at the hall, Jane duly presented her invitation and made her way to the cloakroom to deposit her coat, took a quick look at herself in the mirror to see all was well, and then walked into the brightly lit and gaily decorated hall. The dance was already in full swing, the orchestra playing the latest popular waltz. Jane looked round quickly seeking a familiar face and espying her friend, Babs, further down the room made her way towards her and sat down in the vacant seat beside her.

Mrs Fitzroy, meanwhile, had made her way to the gallery to join the other matrons gathered there and she joined in the general buzz of greetings and small talk. In the centre of the group was Mrs Maloney, a large imposing woman, a leading light socially. The Maloneys were well off, being the owners of the largest haberdashery store on the camp. She also had two very pretty daughters, Ita, a slim girl with glossy black hair, brown eyes and pale olive skin, who was much admired, but not by Mrs Fitzroy, too foreign looking she thought, and she preferred Beth, a blue-eyed redhead. Both girls were always surrounded by a crowd of the young officers and could have their pick of any one of them.

Mrs Maloney was also a snob, well aware of her social position, and did not regard Mrs Fitzroy as of much consequence. After all, was not Mr Fitzroy only a very minor civilian employee of the Military Authorities. Mrs Fitzroy knew full well what Mrs Maloney thought, but in her opinion her Jack was worth ten of Mr Maloney, store or no store.

Jack Fitzroy had been in the army himself and was still a fine figure of a man, tall and straight, with a luxuriant moustache, waxed at the ends. He had seen much service abroad, especially in India, which he loved. He had been in the famous Connaught Rangers and she remembered with pride the day that the Commander-in-Chief, the Duke of Connaught himself, had been inspecting a Guard of Honour and had stopped to have a few words with her husband, asking if he was going to make the army his career. Jack Fitzroy had replied that he would very much like to do so if he was given the opportunity, whereupon the Duke had turned to the Colonel and said "See that this man is taken on again, will you."

So he had done his time and the little pension he had made served them well as their family grew up. He came of a good family but had run away and joined the army in his teens. His father had died when he was very young and he had been an only child. His uncle was his guardian and, rightly or wrongly, he always maintained that his mother had not received proper treatment as regards their share of the property and they lived in very straightened circumstances.

When his mother died he joined the army to see the world and when he left he had taken a job on a large estate, the owner of which was an ex-army man also. The major had position, good connections, a large estate but no money, and, as so often happened in those days, had married it. The lady of the manor was an American.

Jack was given the gatehouse for his young family and Mrs Fitzroy had to open the gates for the gentry in their fine carriages and close them again after them. He had to chop all the wood for the house, pump all the water, provide fresh vegetables and generally help in keeping the gardens and grounds in order. Often there would be large house parties when every bedroom in the huge old mansion would be occupied, and he had to provide all the extra wood for the fires which would be burning in every room, and pump all the extra water for baths for the guests.

It was hard, grinding, unremitting toil from early morning

until late at night, and, though he was a big strong man, he knew that such a pace would soon sap even his strength and vitality. He resolved to find another job and this decision was given even more priority by an incident which occurred one day when he and the major were on an inspection tour of the gardens. The lady of the manor approached the major and asked if he could spare Jack to do a job in the house. The major refused adding the phrase "Can't one of your own tame slaves do it?"

This shocked Jack and he made the mental note that the major would never see the day when one of his daughters was one of those tame slaves. That very night he wrote to his old commanding officer to see if he could get any other work for him, and the result was the job he now occupied on the army camp.

So Jack had gone to give his notice to the major, not without some regret, as though the work had been hard, it was outdoor and suited him, and he and the major had a certain amount of respect for one another, they understood one another. Jack was not afraid of the major, he would say what he thought and stand his ground in face of the general himself if he thought he was in the right.

Then, too, they had been very comfortable in the little gatehouse, and even though the lady of the manor was proud and haughty, if one of his children was ill a basket of fruit and other little luxuries would be sent down, or if his wife was ill, hot nourishing meals were provided from the big house. The major tried very hard to keep Jack, pointing out among other things, that his daughters would have employment, in due course, at the big house, little knowing Jack's private thoughts on that subject. He was determined that none of his daughters would go into service if he could help it, and so he had arranged for Jane and his second daughter, Nan, to be apprenticed to Mrs Fogarty, the dressmaker, and his youngest daughter, Mary, to upholstery. He considered it no less than his duty to do his best for them.

Mrs Fitzroy's thoughts were interrupted at that moment by the arrival of a tall young man who, after a quick look round, made his way towards the happy laughing group which surrounded Beth and Ita. Why, it's him she thought, and indeed it was the very same young man in whom she had often voiced her interest. She turned to Mrs Fogarty and enquired if she knew who he was. Mrs Fogarty did.

"He's Sergeant Charles Sweeney. They say Beth Maloney is very sweet on him!" and indeed at that very moment he was leading Beth on to the floor.

"Oh" said Mrs Fitzroy, somewhat sourly, "I shouldn't have thought a mere sergeant would be good enough for them."

"Well" said Mrs Fogarty "they do say that he was sent home from France to take officer's training course, but the war ended before he finished it." In those days men were not promoted through the ranks in peace-time.

"Still" continued Mrs Fogarty, "I suppose the fact that he was chosen to take the course gives him a certain standing with the Maloneys, and, anyway, as I said, Beth is very sweet on him."

Another pair of eyes had noted the entrance of the young man, Jane's, and her heart sank when she saw him join the crowd round the two Maloney girls.

'Oh, well,' she thought 'that's that! Can't compete with those two!'

She did not lack for partners herself, but the excitement of the evening just fizzled out for her and she realised just how much she had wanted to see him again.

There was a stir at the door and a party of the senior officers made their appearance. Standing in the midst of them was a very arresting figure indeed. This was a young subaltern of the Indian Army, dressed in a strange uniform with a rich silken sash and turban. He seemed to be only about Jane's own age, very tall and slim, with fine chiselled features and an habitually grave countenance occasionally lit up by the brilliance of his smile.

Many stories circulated about this romantic figure. It was said he was a prince in his own country being the son of a fabulously wealthy Rajah. No one knew for sure but it was quite apparent that he was held in high esteem by his brother officers from the commanding officer down.

He stood among his friends, until the band struck up a Viennese waltz, when he left the group and made his way across the floor to where Jane was sitting and, as she knew he would, bowed before her and requested the pleasure of this dance. He led her on to the floor, the centre of all eyes. As they circled gracefully together in time to the beautiful music he talked easily to her in his perfect English putting her at ease, and when the music ended he drew her arm through his and escorted her back to her place. He always danced the Viennese waltz with Jane whenever he saw her at any of the dances and as she said to her mother many times "He may be a prince or he may not be, but he treats me just as though I was a princess."

The band struck up a Veleta and Jane's heart missed a beat as she saw the young man who had invited her standing before her, smiling and asking her to dance. The two of them took the floor.

"It was only when I saw you dancing with Lieutenant Khan just now that I realised you had come" he said. "I hope you haven't promised all your dances!"

"No" said Jane.

"That's good" he said "I would like several more, if you don't object, of course."

Jane could only nod her head happily.

Up in the gallery Mrs Fitzroy was happy too. Her Jane and that handsome young man were dancing together and seemed to be enjoying each other's company very much and when he took her into supper she smiled to herself. She knew that already there was something between them and was content.

Paddy and the Banshee

I well remember the night my Grandfather died. It was about two o'clock in the morning when Gran came into the room to waken my Aunt Mary.

Only half awake I heard her whisper "Get up, May, it's yer father."

Aunt Mary rose quietly and dressed quickly joining Gran in the kitchen. I lay there for a few minutes, but feeling vaguely alarmed by the unusual commotion, I too got out of bed and went to the kitchen where Gran had already lit the big oil lamp and was throwing dry sticks and turf onto the almost burned out fire coaxing it back into life again. She filled the large kettle and put it on the fire. Gran's unfailing remedy in any crisis was always the "sup o' tay".

As soon as she saw me she ran to pick me up off the cold stone kitchen floor on which I was standing in my bare feet. She was for putting me back to bed at once, clucking her tongue and scolding that I would catch my death of cold, but I beseeched her tearfully to let me stay up with her. The thought of returning alone to that big room lit only by the little red lamp burning in front of the picture of the Sacred Heart, and the big bed without Aunt Mary to snuggle into, filled me with terror. So Gran relented, wrapped me in a blanket and sat me in the old rocking-chair in front of the fire, where I sat watching anxiously as Gran and Aunt Mary talked together in whispers.

I was about eight years old at this time and Aunt Mary was about twenty-two, and I thought she was very pretty. She was small and dainty with dark hair, milky skin and blue eyes, a real Irish beauty. She was also very lively with a great sense of fun. We got on well together, in fact we were more like sisters than niece and aunt, not that I ever addressed her as "Aunt" in my life.

At last I heard Gran say "Well there's nothing else for it as Ned's away, ye'll have to go for Biddy Malone yerself." I knew then what had happened. I knew that I would never see my Grandfather again for Biddy Malone was the village woman who would come to prepare for the wake as was the custom of the time.

Aunt Mary was very reluctant to go naturally. It was a dark night with the moon breaking fitfully through fast scudding clouds casting dancing shadows on the road and in the hedges, and the thought of the half mile or so to Biddy's cottage struck fear to her heart; but she had to go, so she got out her bicycle and set off.

She arrived at Biddy's cottage without mishap, and on getting her promise to come as quickly as possible, thankfully set off home again. She had only a short distance to go when she heard an awful clanking, creaking noise coming towards her from around the bend in the road ahead. Her nerves already at breaking point, sheer terror gripped her, and she let out the most terrible blood-curdling shriek, which was immediately followed by a loud clanging crash just ahead. Fear lending her strength she pedalled furiously past the two glittering orbs, and the dark shapeless moaning thing in the middle of the road.

When she got home she threw down her bike and pounded on the door screaming to be let in. Gran, badly frightened, opened the door, whereupon Aunt Mary fell into her arms crying hysterically.

"God bless us and save us, child" said Gran "what in Hiven's name ails ye?" and on managing to calm her down a bit and make some sort of sense of her tale, the three of us huddled together nervously to await Biddy's arrival. Gran, looking as I shall always remember her, in a black dress down to her ankles, her shawl wrapped tightly round her shoulders, hair parted in the middle and drawn up into a bun at the nape of the neck, and those amazingly clear, young, beautiful grey eyes deep set in her brown wrinkled face, sat in the rocking-chair, with me on her lap, telling her beads, with Aunt Mary on the stool close beside us.

Soon we heard Biddy's knock, and Aunt Mary rose quickly and let her in. Biddy was a tiny wisp of a "widda woman" as Gran called her. She was well over seventy but lean and spritely. She always somehow reminded me of a robin. She was brown from head to toe, from her battered old felt hat to her button boots. She had lively, inquisitive brown eyes, apple cheeks and a certain way of putting her head to one side as she talked, just like a robin. Biddy was also much troubled by Aunt Mary's tale and, after doing what she came to do, she resolutely refused to set foot outside until it was light, and so we stayed, drinking hot sweet tea, until the dawn broke, when Biddy departed and we went thankfully to our beds for an hour or two's sleep.

Gradually, as the days passed I started to forget this frightening incident, and I was helped in this when I became aware that my Aunt Mary was "doing a line" with Paddy Penrose. I was intensely interested in the proceedings. I liked Paddy. I liked his dark curling hair and smiling blue eyes. Paddy had a small farm, kept a few cows and had a thriving little business delivering milk to all the nearby villages. He delivered the milk by pony and cart, driving furiously between stops, standing upright, legs straddled with the reins in one hand and cracking a whip loudly over the pony's ears with the other, for all the world as though he imagined himself to be Ben Hur in his chariot, bringing the pony to a precipitous stop precisely opposite our gate. Many a time as I waited for him, jug in hand, I had the fear, or could it just possibly be the wicked hope, that Paddy would one day misjudge the pony's pace and take a flying nosedive into the muddy ditch by our gate.

No matter what the weather was like Paddy always had a cheerful greeting.

"Foine mornin' that be, Mam" he would say to Gran "foine mornin' indade bedad, thank God", or "Turrible blowy wind that be this mornin', Mam, turrible blowy weather altogether, but thank God", and if it was a wet day "Turrible wettin' rain this, Mam, turrible wettin', but thank God for it just the same."

Gran often tasted the milk very suspiciously as she vowed he was not above adding a pint or two of water to the churn if he thought he might run short.

On many an evening now Paddy would drop in for a few yarns and I would watch Aunt Mary as she bustled about making the tea, rather pink cheeked and giggly under Paddy's admiring eye. Paddy was very generous to me. He always had something for me, a couple of pence maybe or a bar of chocolate or a few sweets, and once, for some reason I never knew, he gave me a whole half-crown, an awful lot of money in those days, and when I excitedly showed it to Gran, she took it from me saying that it was too much to give me altogether, and the next time he pressed a shining sixpence into my hand and whispered that if I had any sense at all I would say nothing about it.

Then one evening after Paddy had emptied his third cup of tea and had helped himself liberally to Gran's delicious home-made currant bread, he told us of the night he had heard the banshee.

"Oh, yes, 'twas the banshee all right" said Paddy thoroughly enjoying our rapt attention. "I had a few jars in Andy Flynn's and after yarnin' for a while, I picked up me empty cans, slung them over the crossbar and set off home. I had just passed the crossroads by the bend in the road when I heard her screetching like a soul in torment, and then she flew past me in a blast of icy air. I'm not the bether of it yet, I can tell ye, nor will I be for many a day" said Paddy. "An' twas that very same night that yer father, God rest him, passed away May."

We sat in silence for a few minutes looking nervously at one another. Then Aunt Mary said in a thoughtful voice "That was me!"

"What" said Paddy startled.

"That was me ye heard" said Aunt Mary even more thoughtfully, and then, as the full realisation dawned on her, she jumped up and shouted at the still gaping Paddy.

"That was me ye heard, me, ye auld omadthaun. I'd bin to get Biddy Malone to lay out me father. Ye frightened the life out av me with yer auld creakin' bike and clankin' cans, roamin' the roads when all dacent Christians should be abed. Banshee indade" she said witheringly.

Paddy still sat shocked into immobility trying to take it all in and when at last he did he also jumped up and shouted back at Aunt Mary just as furiously.

"I frightened the life out av ye, did I? An' what do ye think ye did to me with yer fiendish screetchin'. Ye put the fear av God inta me I can tell ye! Faith an' a real banshee couldn't have done any bether!"

He grabbed up his cap and rushed off without another word, and that, alas, spelled the end of what to my mind at any rate, had all the makings of a very beautiful friendship indeed.

The Last Christmas

As the days shortened, Kathleen and I would go blackberrying
and I would help Gran to make delicious blackberry jelly, and
blackberry and apple jam, as someone would be sure to give us
some apples. I always loved gathering things, mushrooms;
crab-apples; beech nuts; elderberries, which I made into ink;
and sloes, so sour that they would take every bit of juice from
your mouth, leaving it like emery paper. Most people made
wine from elderberries and sloes but we never made wine. We
were all teetotal in our house, in fact Gran had a horror of "the
dhrink" though I have been told that Grandfather "in his young
day" liked a drop or two. In fact he would sometimes go on a
right old binge, then get thoroughly ashamed of himself, take
the pledge for a year, and when the year was up, having rigidly
adhered to his word, he would go on another binge, and
repeat the process.

After Halloween, which was a great night for merrymaking,
as gangs of young people with blackened faces, and dressed in
outlandish style, carrying candles in hollowed out turnips,
thundered at the door and feasted on all the good things laid
out for them before moving on to the next house, the roads
resounding to their singing and laughter, there was Christmas
to look forward to. There were cakes to be made, and
puddings to be made. Kathleen and I took a trip to a nearby
wood to gather our holly and with a bit of luck sometimes a
sprig or two of mistletoe, never venturing in too far, as it was

dark and forbidding-looking and we were nervous we would get lost.

That year was the year that I fell in love for the first time. I was twelve years old. The boy was about sixteen and came from a very wealthy farming family. They did not attend the village school but he, and his brothers and sisters, travelled by pony and trap to a much better school several miles distant in the nearest small town.

The family lived in a huge old mansion, set back about half a mile from the road, the only access to which was through an open field via a rough track, the gate to which bore a large sign "Beware of the Bull". Needless to say their contact with the village children was nil.

Every morning as I trudged to school I was overtaken by the pony and trap, the occupants of which at first sailed past with eyes straight ahead, completely ignoring me, but gradually they stole shy glances, then smiled and called greetings. Then one day the boy pulled up the pony and asked me if I would like a lift. I was completely taken aback, it was so unexpected, but when the youngest child, a boy of about six, opened the trap door invitingly and beckoned, I climbed in and wedged myself into the small space available. I was rather self-conscious and tongue-tied as six pairs of eyes focused on me very intently, but, gradually as the boy made a habit of stopping each morning, I lost my shyness and was soon chattering away in answer to their questions.

My school friends were jealous. He had never given anyone a lift before, and indeed I was conscious of a feeling of wonder that a tall, handsome lad like him could be at all interested in me, small, skinny townie that I was. But interested he most certainly was, plying me with questions about myself, my life in Glasgow, and my family.

I thought of the boy constantly. I hated Saturday and Sunday when I did not see him, and the ten minutes or so that I spent in his company each morning were the high spot of my day. Then one morning he just passed by without so much as a glance as I turned round expectantly on hearing the pony's clip-clop on the road. Bewildered and hurt I continued on my way presently being joined by one of my class-mates.

"No lift this mornin' I see" she said maliciously. "Ye know

Tom, me brother, works up at the farm and he says they've all been havin' great sport imitatin' everythin' ye've said in that awful Glasgow accent av yourn."

We always had a goose for Christmas, and on that last Christmas our goose was ready, plucked and stuffed, as Gran and Uncle Ned prepared to set out for Midnight Mass. Aunt Mary, of course, was home for Christmas and it had been decided that she and I would go to morning Mass on Christmas Day. I dearly wanted to go to Midnight Mass with Gran but for some reason she would not let me go that year. I loved the midnight service, and I knew everyone would be there if at all possible. It was about three miles to our little parish church but the roads would be filled with happy cheerful people and the way did not seem long. Gran usually got a lift from Mrs Riley who would set out from the farm with the trap full of young Rileys and as they caught up with one of Mrs Riley's cronies, such as Gran, one by one they would be turned out to make room in the trap.

Uncle Ned, of course, usually came with us to Midnight Mass and once Gran was established in Mrs Riley's trap along with as many of the older women as it would carry, he would put me on the crossbar and we would follow on behind.

But one Christmas that I remember well, Uncle Ned did not come with us for some reason. It was a cold frosty moonlit night as Gran and I set out together and Kathleen joined me when Mrs Riley pulled up to lift Gran.

After Mass, Gran accepted the offer of a lift home on receiving Mrs Riley's assurance that Pat, her eldest boy, would see me safely home. Pat was not too keen to say the least. It was not that it was all that much out of his way, no, the real objection for Pat was the fact that we would have to pass an old graveyard and, horror of horrors, he would have to pass it alone on his way back. Poor Pat was quite terrified of the dark, a fact which was well known, and the subject of much teasing, by the rest of the family, who would relate with glee the story of the night that Pat walking home from a friend's, had become aware of something the other side of the hedge keeping pace with him, and as he started to run the thing also quickened pace and broke out into a blood-curdling scream. Such was his terror that he burst into the house not bothering to undo the latch, just broke it open with his shoulder, galloped upstairs and into bed leaving Mrs Riley to go down and bolt the door after him, asserting loudly that it was no more than a vixen on the prowl.

Another night he had been cycling home when suddenly a large black creature with blazing eyes and panting horribly appeared at his side and kept pace no matter how he tried to shake it off, and when he hysterically burst into the brightly lit kitchen trying to tell his story, one of their own black mongrels appeared in the lighted doorway. Pat, of course, was not at all convinced by those logical explanations.

There were several hazards to be passed on the way home but with such good company it did not matter, still the thought would creep in just the same. There was the old sandpit from whence a very large headless man was wont to leap out on lone and unwary late night travellers; the spot where two trees were joined together in such a peculiar way as to make a natural gibbet which was reputed to have been used for that very purpose on more than one occasion in past days; the blackened shell of a burnt out cottage where a young and demented mother was forever trying to save her little one who perished in the flames; but the worst one of all was the graveyard.

It was an old graveyard, long disused, but still well tended, approached by a long tree-lined drive. The tiny church, still used occasionally by the sparse Church of Ireland congregation of the district, stood on a hill and could be clearly seen outlined against the sky, especially on moonlit nights. Into a high curved wall were set the massive entrance gates, and it was against these gates that the figure of a young man, dressed in dark clothes of a bygone age, with the moonlight playing on the elegant silver buckles of his shoes, was often said to have been seen in an attitude of great grief sobbing to himself.

As we trudged along people gradually dropped off until there were only Pat, Kathleen and Mick Riley and me left in our little group. There were still little knots of people laughing and talking both ahead and behind, and when we came to the parting of our ways Kathleen and Mick refused all Pat's pleas to accompany me to my door, so there was nothing left for Pat to do but hurry me along as quickly as he could and when we came to the graveyard he flatly refused to go a step further and bade me run to catch up with the group ahead. This I did, and as I sped along I could hear Pat pounding along in the opposite direction in the hope of catching up the other two, a vain hope I would say, as, if I knew anything of their impish sense of humour, the instant we were out of sight the two of them took to their heels.

Although we all laughed at Pat, there was not one of us who did not believe in ghosts and I can remember Gran relating a tale about my Grandfather, who was by no means a fanciful man, having some sort of an encounter which affected him very much and it happened this way.

They had not long been married when a message arrived at their cottage asking if he would go to the presbytery to see the parish priest. When he arrived the old man told him he had to go out on a sick call to an outlying village and would my Grandfather accompany him. Grandfather was quite willing to do so. In common with everyone else he knew why.

Some years before the old priest had been called to effect an exorcism in one of the larger houses in the parish. The story ran that a long time ago there had been some manifestation in the house which had terrified the inhabitants and a previous parish priest had managed to confine the malevolent presence to one room, which had been sealed up and thereafter the disturbances ceased. The years passed and several generations later, the new heir had pooh-poohed all efforts to dissuade him and opened the door of the room which he then proceeded to prepare for use.

Soon the disturbances started again and reached such proportions that the young man was obliged to seek the aid of the clergy once more. Ever since that time the old priest refused to go out alone at night and, if he had to do so for any reason, one of the young men of the parish was persuaded to accompany him. On that night something happened that frightened my Grandfather very much, but neither he nor the old priest ever talked about just what it was. The young man who had been the cause of all the trouble was given the penance of having to pay a visit to the parish church on every day of his life thereafter, and not long afterwards, as he was returning from one of these visits, he was found dead on the road without any outward sign on him to explain why.

As I was smiling to myself at the memory of that night, Gran bustled into the kitchen all dressed ready to go and she said to Aunt Mary "Now, May, remember what I told ye! Don't go scrubbin' the floor, it's clane enough, an' no haulin' and pullin' out the furniture nayther. We don't want the place all upset Christmas mornin'!"

Aunt Mary nodded but as soon as Gran and Uncle Ned were safely on their way, she set to work. She got a bucket and the scrubbing brush and a big bar of carbolic soap, and started on the kitchen floor. She pulled out all the furniture, got into every nook and cranny, scrubbing furiously. Then she mopped it dry as well as she could, put back the cupboards and chairs in exactly the same position, washed her hands thoroughly, surveyed her handiwork with evident satisfaction and said "Now, Jen, you and me'll have a nice cup av cocoa and a wedge of home-made," and she put on fresh water in the big black kettle and when it boiled she made the cocoa and we sat sipping and chatting together. Aunt Mary anxiously inspected the floor from time to time to see how well it was drying as she wanted no trace left as she said "No wan'll be anny the wiser, Jen, only yerself and meself!"

Aunt Mary hated dirt, and insisted on scrubbing and cleaning until there was not a speck to be seen and the whole place was in complete chaos. On the other hand Gran was very quick but thorough. I never saw Gran anything but neat and tidy or flurried about the housework, and the place was always well kept. She would go into the sitting-room and rearrange a little ornament or two, reposition a bowl of flowers, a few cushions, and with a little tweak here and a little tweak there, somehow the room would look immeasurably more attractive.

Aunt Mary banked up the fire yet again until we had to move well back from it, in an effort to speed up the drying, which was much too slow for her liking. Then, as she bound up my hair in rags in preparation for the morrow, she had an idea and ran to get the two heavy irons from the cupboard, placed them on the range to heat, rummaged for as much old bits of sheeting as she could find, put them down on the floor and proceeded to iron over them to get as much of the damp up as she could.

Finally, deciding that perhaps discretion was the better part, we went to bed as she muttered "Better make ourselves scarce, Jen! from the looks av that floor it won't be dry till New Year!"

The next morning, we were up bright and early to cycle to Christmas Day Mass and no mention was made of the floor. We returned to a beautiful smell of roasting goose permeating the whole cottage, Christmas pudding bubbling away merrily on the range, and soon we were all sitting down to a succulent plateful and after Grace I was just about to put a large forkful of goose in my mouth, when Aunt Mary suddenly jumped up exclaiming agitatedly that she could not remember what she had done with the needle she had used to sew up the carcase after stuffing it, worrying whether it was still in the goose and urging us all to be very careful in case we swallowed it.

"Arrah" said Uncle Ned crossly "trust ye to do something like that" and we all poked about carefully, scrutinising every mouthful thereafter.

That was the last Christmas I spent with Gran as soon after Easter I travelled over to England to join my family in a completely new way of life and commence preparations in earnest for my future.

"Oh Bad, Bad Man!"

I soon settled down at my new school, a small private convent school, as my parents felt I would receive more individual attention in an effort to recover some of the ground I had lost as regards my standard of education during the previous couple of years. I stayed there about eighteen months and then moved on to a secretarial college to train for my chosen profession, shorthand typist.

Hannah had not yet started school, but Jack, of course, had been attending the local primary for a couple of years and had made his first conquest, a little damsel who was to be the first of many to succumb to Jack's attraction. His fair hair had now turned a light golden brown but his blue eyes were still dancing with the love of "divillment" as Gran would call it, as much as ever. To Jack's extreme annoyance she would knock for him each morning and ask my mother "Is your brother coming to school?" and Jack would have to do what my mother bade him and escort her there safely, and the two of them would walk along together with Jack keeping to the very edge of the pavement in order to keep as much space as possible between them in the hope that his pals would not think they were together.

One morning my father answered her knock and she asked the same question "Is your brother coming to school?" whereupon my father answered gravely that he was but that he was not quite ready and whilst they were waiting he asked her what her name was.

"Rosemary" she replied.

"Rosemary" said my father "that is a nice name! What's your other name?"

"Ann" she replied.

"That's nice too," said my father, "but I meant your last name, your surname."

"Oh" she said airily, "I haven't got one of those. My brother has one, but I haven't."

My father laughed as Jack appeared at that moment, and he watched the two of them wander up the road.

One wet day Jack was bored as he was unable to get out, so my mother gave him a duster and told him to dust the living-room, and after that he could polish the table "and don't forget to put a bit of elbow grease into it" she said, "and then I'll be able to get on with your favourite dinner, steak and kidney pie."

Jack took the duster and the polish and cloth and disappeared into the living-room and after a while, thinking he was very quiet and wondering what he was up to, my mother sneaked in to have a peep to see Jack vigorously polishing the table with his elbow firmly stuck in a little nest he had made with the duster.

She tiptoed quietly away.

As soon as the dinner was ready, I laid the table and we all sat down. The pie smelled delicious, and we soon had a generous portion set before each of us. Jack's only grumble was that he had to stretch to get everything he wanted as he was at the far end of the table.

"I wish I was Ping the Elastic Man" he said "then I'd only have to put out my arm and it would reach to the very end of the table."

"Ping the Elastic Man" was one of Jack's favourite stories of the moment, in his weekly adventure booklet.

My mother soon became aware of Hannah who had not touched her dinner.

"What's the matter, Hannah?" she asked. "Eat up it's very tasty."

Hannah shook her head and pushed the plate away. "Don't want any" she said.

"Here" said my father, "take this spoonful it's good for you" proferring a small spoonful to her.

"No" screamed Hannah pushing it violently away. "Don't want any. I won't eat any of that snake. I won't, I won't!"

And not a mouthful would she touch despite all our explanations and assurances.

We had a small tabby cat at this time. My mother was never too fond of animals but it was Hannah's especial pet so was tolerated and Hannah loved it passionately and Kitty returned this affection in full measure. As soon as Hannah sat down Kitty would leap on to her lap and sit there with one paw on each shoulder gazing up into her face adoringly, purring loudly as she stroked her. She loathed Jack as much as she loved Hannah, he was such a tease, and would take a flying leap to the top of the coal shed whenever she heard him approaching, and when she saw Kitty glaring down the alleyway my mother would grin and say "That must be Jack now!"

Every cat in the neighbourhood would be viciously chased off with the exception of a large black Tom, and when her kittens arrived there was always at least one black one amongst them. She favoured these black ones quite blatantly, many a time when we had them in to play she would cuff the ears of the poor little tabby kittens, but she never touched the black ones, which she would cuddle and groom fondly.

It was always a traumatic time for us when we had to part with the kittens and each time my mother would vow that Kitty would have to go, she was too much of a nuisance; but she did not really mean it.

Jack's favourite trick was to load his water pistol and go in search of Kitty, saucer of milk in hand to entice her out of whatever hiding-place she had found for herself amongst the flowers and shrubs, calling in his cajoling way "Here, Kitty, Kitty. Here, Kitty, Kitty" and when she had unwisely taken the bait, producing the water pistol from behind his back where he had kept it hidden and squirting furiously.

Immediately opposite us there lived a lady whom we always called Mrs Jumbo. We never knew what her real name was. She had an old, black dog, of which she was very fond, and several times a day we would hear the cry "Here Jumbo. Here Jumb Jumb."

One day when Jack was up to his usual tricks in our front garden he suddenly heard a voice crying "You naughty, naughty, boy" and looked up to see Mrs Jumbo glaring furiously at him over the hedge. Jack beat a hasty retreat up the alleyway, and thereafter he confined himself to our back garden.

August Bank Holiday was always the bank holiday of the year for us and I shall never forget one when our cousins and Aunt Jane and Uncle Charles came to visit. We set out early for Hampstead Heath where there was always a huge fair and sideshows and shooting galleries, for which my father and Uncle Charles made a bee-line at once. We had a great time sampling everything we could afford. "The Haunted House" was last on the agenda and my mother disgraced herself by screaming blue murder to be let out almost as soon as we entered. She did not mind the skeletons, spooks and ghostly apparitions appearing in her path, no, it was the cobwebby, dangling things brushing her face in the pitch-black which sent her into hysterics. By the time we got her out she was almost fainting but, I am afraid, she got scant sympathy from the rest of us who all thought it was a great lark.

The next day we visited some of the landmarks in London, the National Gallery where once again our visit was cut short when we had to rush Hannah out "toot sweet" as my father said, airing his French, when she got an attack of "seasickness" from continually moving her head up and down viewing the pictures.

Then it was on to "Madame Tussauds" the most eagerly awaited event for my cousins as it was their first visit. We, of course, had been before and we had great fun with the distorting mirrors and Jack got the usual laugh by dispatching my cousins to ask the way to the Chamber of Horrors from the "policeman" at the foot of the stairs. Henry the Eighth and all his wives drew us like a magnet and we clustered in front of them eagerly discussing all the ladies and their gowns and jewels.

"She must have been the last one" said Hannah pointing.

"Why must she?" asked Jack.

"Well, she's got all the best jewels on" said Hannah, and so she had, which makes Hannah's remark a valid one.

G

We soon became aware that we had a very interested listener, a tiny smiling old lady, who appeared to be Japanese.

"Excuse please" she said "no much English" and she held up six fingers and said "Six marrieds?"

"Yes" said Jack "six marrieds."

She ran her finger down the list "What that mean?" she asked pointing to the word "beheaded".

"He cut off her head" said Jack.

She shrugged uncomprehendingly.

"He cut off her head" said Jack again and caught hold of Hannah and demonstrated.

"Oh, bad man" she said and when she came to the second "beheaded" and looked at us, Jack laughed, and as he prepared to demonstrate once more, she looked horrified and crying "Bad, bad man" to herself she scampered off.

We moved on and were about to join Aunt Jane and my mother when Jack stopped us and said "Will you just look at those two!" and we looked and saw them closely inspecting a figure reclining very comfortably in a chair with a white peaked cap pulled down well over his eyes. It was in the section devoted to "Sportsmen" and Aunt Jane was peering into the face and saying "This is the best one yet. It's awful real looking!"

"Yes," said my mother "but who is it?" And they continued poking about on the floor looking for the nameplate.

Suddenly, to their complete horror, the face started to crumple and soon the figure was rolling about in convulsions of silent mirth. They looked at him for a few moments before beating a hurried retreat, covered in confusion, with Aunt Jane saying "I suppose we'll never hear the end of this" and my mother replying "No suppose about it, you can bank on that!"

When he had recovered himself somewhat the perpetrator of the hoax came up to us to apologise. He turned out to be an American tourist who said he just could not resist the temptation.

Aunt Jane and my mother were somewhat mollified by this courteous gesture saying that it was his white cap which had misled them, they had thought he was a golfer perhaps, but it was no use because soon we were all laughing heartily together once more, and indeed, for long after every time we thought of it we laughed until the tears flowed.

The War Years

I started my first job as a junior shorthand typist in the summer of 1939. It was at a large railway depot on the outskirts of London but our particular section was quite small. There were only three typists; Hetty, in charge, was in her twenties, which of course, seemed quite old to me; then there was Vi about eighteen; and myself, sixteen.

The war which had been threatening for so long finally came on September 3rd, 1939, but the war really started for me on Friday, September 1st, when Poland was invaded. Emergency plans must have been in preparation for some time because suddenly there was a flurry of activity, re-routing schedules, re-rostering of guards and drivers, evacuation plans to be catered for, and the three of us were kept going at full stretch until quite late on that Friday evening. Once Poland had been invaded, and as we had a pact to go to their aid, war was now inevitable. At last I was told to go home and report again on the morrow, Saturday, which I was very glad to do, but on leaving the office I got a great shock, I walked out into total blackness not a light to be seen anywhere. Was it a trial blackout? I did not know. I did know I was petrified as I felt my way along by the railings until I came to the station entrance where there were more people about. The ticket collector and the booking clerk were working inside with only the light of a flickering candle. There was not a light on the platform, not a light on the train. Gradually of course, as the eyes got accustomed to the darkness different objects could be picked out. People were smoking, their lighted cigarettes casting a small glow, and as I shuffled along feeling carefully for the steps down to the platform, I felt my arm grabbed and a cheerful voice said "Here, love, hang on to me" and someone took hold of the other arm, and a couple more joined on, and we made our way slowly down the steps on to the platform and when the train came in, we somehow or other scrambled into a compartment. I had only a couple of stops to go so knew exactly where I was but there were quite a few accidents as confused passengers mistook their station, opened the compartment doors on the wrong side and fell on the line, despite the station staffs' valiant efforts to run along the train shouting the name of the station. I safely negotiated the platform, the stairs, and got through the barrier and into the booking-hall, lit once again by the light of a candle, and all the time I was dreading the half mile walk to my home.

Then a figure came out of the gloom and I heard a voice say "Hullo Jen" and I looked up to see Jim Saunders, one of the clerks from the office, and I felt a deep rush of gratitude as he took my arm and said "Just thought I'd hang on and see you safely home." I was never more glad to see anyone in my life.

I had only had a very casual acquaintance with Jim before that night but afterwards, of course, we became a twosome.

Sunday, September 3rd, my birthday, I remember vividly. Immediately after listening to Mr Chamberlain's broadcast informing the nation that we were now at war, I heard the banshee wail of the air raid warning siren for the first time and the street resounded to the sound of whistles as Air Raid Wardens ran up and down warning everyone to take cover. Where did they come from? They just seemed to pop up out of nowhere, complete with tin hats, gas masks and full uniform. In common with everyone else I expected to be blown sky-high within the hour.

It did not happen, of course, and during the twelve months grace that followed life changed considerably. I was in a "reserved" occupation, that is I would not be called up, but all my friends either joined the women's forces, or went into war production, as gradually the factories changed over into working for the war effort.

My mother took a part time job in a supply depot for airmen's clothing; my father first joined the Home Guard as an Instructor, then became a radio operator at a Government Monitoring Station, thus releasing a younger man for active service. Jim, who had already taken training, became an Air Raid Warden until such time as he was called up for the regiment of his choice, and which I privately thought a very posh one, The Life Guards.

The next few months were happy ones as Jim squired me to the dances and the pictures and exciting days too as London gradually filled up with servicemen of all nationalities. I particularly enjoyed it when Jim took me up to the West End, Jim immaculate in sports coat and flannels, me in my best navy edge-to-edge coat, flowered dress underneath, with the little bunch of violets which Jim always bought me from one of the many flower girls pinned to my shoulder, as we strolled in the parks, window-shopped or joined the queues for the cinema or a show.

At work too it was an exciting time. We had to take part in regular air raid drills; learn how to use a stirrup pump to put out incendiaries, with water flying everywhere; and practise typing with our gas masks on in case of a gas attack. This was quite a feat as they were of the canister type, the eye pieces of which misted up, and when we leaned forward to see better, the end banged on the typewriter causing us to giggle, and when we giggled the escaping air made a loud raspberry, causing more giggles and louder raspberries. The sight of the chief clerk peering through the glass window of the door to our room, checking to see we were carrying out instructions, and wearing his own gas mask which was of the more sophisticated type which made him appear like some huge ant, caused near hysterics and gargantuan raspberries.

Oh, yes, it all seemed a great lark to me to begin with, but as time went on and all the young men in the office joined up and went away, some never to return, and then the not so young men also, and their places were taken by women, the news seemed only to be of reverses and then came Dunkirk, which created a great sense of shock and disbelief. The next morning word flew round the office that a train full of men rescued from the beaches had pulled up for a short stop on the platform immediately underneath our office, and everyone clubbed together and dashed to the kiosks for fags for the lads, crammed into the compartments, tired, dirty but not subdued. I was often teased by the lads in the office "Sweet seventeen and never been kissed" they would say, to my great confusion, but I got a few kisses that day as I ran along the train handing out the cigarettes until one young soldier, who hardly looked much older than myself, with a shock of fair hair standing up in a cow's lick and very blue eyes, caught hold of my hand and refused to let go, putting his other arm round my neck and resting his tired-looking face against mine, and as the train started to pull out I had to run alongside until it picked up speed and then I stood watching as he leaned out the window blowing kisses until he was out of sight, but not out of mind. That young-old face stayed in my memory for many a day. Years later I often thought of that incident at the sight of the hundreds of Italian prisoners of war lined up on the platform each evening awaiting their train back to camp after a day's work, silent and resigned looking, and I felt the same surge of sympathy. I think most people felt the same, I never heard any expression of animosity towards them at any rate.

A few days before Jim was due to join up he took me, as he had long promised to do, to see 'Gone With The Wind'. There had been a great deal of advance publicity about the picture and the long search for the actress to play the coveted part of Scarlett O'Hara, and, as Vivien Leigh and Clark Gable were among my favourites, I looked forward to it immensely. I was not disappointed. Jim and I sat enthralled as the story unfolded before our eyes. To have seen that great film; presented to its best advantage in a first-class cinema; to have experienced the wave of excited anticipation that swept through the audience as the film commenced; I knew would be one of the events in my life that I would never forget.

When we emerged from the cinema we went in search of coffee and a sandwich, and as we settled ourselves, Jim asked, "Well, Jen?"

"It was wonderful, Jim" I said. "Thank you for bringing me!"

Jim sat looking at me very quizzically.

"What is it?" I asked.

"You know, Jen, you look quite a bit like Scarlett O'Hara."

I laughed "Oh if only I did" I said.

"Yes, you do" said Jim. "I think it's the way you do your hair, parted that way in the middle, tied up with your red ribbon, with the curls falling over your ears."

I laughed again and said "Well, now I'll tell you something. I've always thought you had a great look of Cary Grant about you!"

It was Jim's turn to laugh now.

"Well all I can say is that we must make a very handsome couple, don't you?" he said.

I missed Jim a lot when he went away, but as time went on we both changed. Jim certainly changed a great deal over the next couple of years, his experiences made him mature much more quickly than I did, my circumstances not altering so drastically in so short a time, and, we just drifted apart. Jim survived the war, but never returned to the office, staying in the army and making it his career.

I shall always remember Jim with very great affection, he was so kind and thoughtful always, and number those days as amongst the happiest of my life.

At the end of that summer the war really started in earnest with the bombing of the docks in London, and we regarded the distant red glow with horror. In the morning as I went to work I would meet the weary firemen returning to base to prepare for the following night's bombardment. In common with our neighbours we had an Anderson shelter fixed up in the garden but we could not stick it long, it was so cold and uncomfortable, so dark and the thought of all the creepy crawlies was horrifying. I preferred the street shelter which was fitted with bunks so more comfortable; but after a while these too were not occupied much, still it was comforting that they were there if things got a little too hot.

Vi and I soon became best friends, and by a very fortunate coincidence we also lived near one another, a circumstance which was to prove a boon as during the coming years we braved the blackout, dense fogs, and the ever present risk of an air raid, to attend the dances and film shows.

We were both avid film fans, and there were three picture houses in our local High Street, and quite often we would go to all three in a week. It was our major source of entertainment, and what value we got for our money. We could get in for as little as 9d. with seats further back for 1/3d. and 1/9d. for the back rows, and 2/3d. for a plush seat in the balcony; and we would see the main film, a supporting film, which quite often I enjoyed more than the main feature, news, and a cartoon. The performance was continuous so if you wanted to you could see the whole programme through twice.

I particularly liked a good "weepie" and there were many of them, but the one I most particularly remember was 'How Green Was My Valley' the story of a mining family in Wales. Vi and I cried from beginning to end and emerged into broad daylight, with splitting headaches, swollen eyes and red noses, still dabbing our faces with sodden hankies.

Some joker in the long waiting queue shouted out "Well it's plain to see you two had a luvly time!"

"Take no notice" hissed Vi, as we ran the gauntlet of that laughing, good-natured crowd, with as much dignity as we could muster.

Vi, on the other hand, had an absolute fascination with horror movies and would beg me to accompany her to any that came round. When 'Dr Jekyl and Mr Hyde' came nothing would do her but to go, and this time we emerged into total blackout. As time went on some form of subdued lighting was introduced on the main roads, but that time had not then arrived. The two of us linked arms tightly, both as jumpy as cats on hot bricks, and my nerves were not improved by Vi continually turning round and peering over her shoulder muttering "I could swear I heard that Hyde panting along behind us!" We were almost home and breathing sighs of relief when, seemingly from nowhere, a large figure loomed up in front of us and peered right into Vi's face. She let out a shriek of terror, whereupon the figure jumped back and a voice said "Oh, sorry, sorry! Silly thing to do! Didn't mean to frighten you! Thought it was my wife and daughter, meeting them you know!" and beat a hasty retreat into the darkness once more. "Well, that settles it" said Vi when she had recovered somewhat "no matter how I beg you in the future, don't ever let me go to a horror film again, never, ever again!"

I smiled to myself at this parting shot from Vi as I well knew that tonight's fright would be forgotten next time a creepy film came round, and I remembered Vi making the very same remark one night when we had been to see a film about werewolves, which I thought rather hilarious, but which had Vi on the edge of her seat biting her nails. I had quite a job to calm her down and had to see her to her door and wait until her father opened it before I could speed on to my own house.

Even fog did not stop us from sallying forth to the pictures if there was something on that we particularly wanted to see. At least on foggy nights we knew that there was no threat of air raids and I remember one night when we optimistically set off hoping that the damp mist would not develop into the thick fog that was forecast. As the evening progressed, however, it got worse and worse, so much so that it got into the cinema and a yellowish swirling curtain soon made it almost impossible to see the screen at all. When we came out it was really bad, but we managed fairly well whilst we were on the main street, with all lights full on, and with such traffic as had been unfortunate enough to be caught in it, crawling along the kerbs, and the odd bus also with the conductor walking ahead holding a bright torch to enable the driver to proceed to the sanctuary of the garage. When we turned off the main road, however, where there was no lighting, the fog descended on us literally as though a blanket had been thrown over our heads. It was a most frightening experience, we lost all sense of direction walking into trees on the grass verges, crossing roads we did not wish to cross and it was only the fact that we were so familiar with the way that enabled us to get home at all that night, and when we did, we were black, black with the filthy, wet, thick, choking smog.

There was another evening when we were at the pictures which I will always remember also. It was during the time when the air raid sirens were wailing on and off almost continuously. At night one plane would circle round and round, keeping everyone awake, and then as its fuel got low, it would drop its load of bombs and another plane would take its place. They kept this up all night, night after night, truly a war of nerves. We backed on to a railway line and there was an anti-aircraft gun mounted on a wagon which travelled up and down firing at them. We viewed this with mixed feelings because, although on the one hand we felt we would like to be able to fly up and

H

claw the thing out of the sky with our bare hands; on the other we felt that it drew attention to us and the shrapnel from the bursting shells constituted quite a hazard and did a lot of damage to roofs etc. Anyway, the gun was taken away and thereafter the planes, and we always knew whether it was a German one or not because of its peculiar engine sound, not a steady drone but rather an uneven one, could do as they pleased.

During the day too the siren would wail on and off all the time, so much so that you would forget whether it was on or off, and it was soon decided that such disruption could not continue, hardly any work at all was getting done, and a "spotter" was placed on the roof so that only in the event of imminent danger would a warning to take cover be given.

This "spotter" was usually a member of the office Home Guard which most of the remaining men had joined and seemed to thoroughly enjoy, with hilarious tales of training with brooms etc. In fact one irate wife had caused a lot of merriment when she had telephoned to demand if her husband was the only member as he was on duty every evening, or so he told her.

One day during this period, Vi came in furious after she fell headlong over the chief clerk as he lay prone in the corridor along with most of the other men after a series of ominous bangs which we had failed to hear because of the clatter of our typewriters, and she called out loudly "Well that's right! Don't nobody bother to tell us there's a raid on, will you?" as they very sheepishly picked themselves up.

Later on, of course, we had the doodle-bugs with their terrifying wait between the engine cut-out and the following crash. Sometimes they would glide silently for miles and descend completely without warning, and I remember hearing once that one of them had glided many miles in this way and landed smack bang in the middle of an American army camp early on a Sunday morning. I don't know whether that was true or not. A lot of news was censored but I do remember that the devastation of the first V2 was explained away as a gas mains explosion.

However, on this particular evening we were sitting in a nearly full cinema enjoying the programme when the air raid siren wailed, and soon there was a faint crump in the distance, then another and another, getting nearer and nearer, and then a loud crash very near indeed. Panic broke out, everyone jumped up and started to rush for the exits. Vi and I also jumped up with the intention of getting out of the large building as quickly as possible, when we were suddenly grabbed from behind and we turned round to see two young sergeants in army battledress who shouted to us to stay in our seats, we would be much safer. Then they ran up and down the aisles shouting the same message. Most people obeyed their orders and stayed where they were, and the next crump was a little further away and the next further still, and soon the "All Clear" sounded for which we felt profound relief. There is no doubt those two young men prevented a very nasty situation from developing that night.

On the way out we passed the two of them as they were receiving the thanks of the manager and patrons and we smiled ours also. As we made our way along the street we could hear footsteps behind us, and then cheerful whistling in time to our steps, and then a voice called out "What's your hurry, girls?" We took no notice and would not turn round for the world. Suddenly there was the sound of running feet, the owner of which was soon beside us taking a good look at us both. He was a lad of about sixteen, and he called out to his friend still behind "Two old hags they are!" in a tone of disgusted disappointment. He ran off fast as Vi made a lunge at him still voicing his disappointment loudly, but he was not half as disappointed as Vi and I for we had been full sure it was the two dashing sergeants following us.

As well as the cinema, we often went roller-skating and we both loved to dance. As time went on we ventured further afield, and one evening as we were travelling by Tube train to a little club where a mixture of modern, square dances, and lively Irish jigs and reels were played, and where we usually had an enjoyable time, we became aware of a young man, good-looking enough in a dark foreign way, taking a very keen interest in us. He seemed to be a seaman of some sort, wore a navy reefer coat, but no flash denoting country of origin, perhaps a merchant seaman we thought. We became a little uneasy under his close scrutiny, and as we approached our stop Vi whispered "Don't hop up until the last minute. We don't want him following us!" We got out just in time before the doors closed only to see the man also leave the train by another door behind us. We hurried along as quickly as we could through the crowded platform, through the barrier, dashed up a side street, and into the club, glad to join the cheerful crowd around the floor and listen to the lilting accordion music the band was playing.

Vi was already dancing when I felt a hand on my arm and turned to see the young man from the train standing beside me and making an obvious invitation to me to dance. We made our way on to the floor where, to my horror, I found that he had absolutely no idea of how to dance, just hopped around me in circles. I wished the music would stop so I could leave the floor, and then my eyes alighted on Vi who was absolutely doubled up with laughter, and to my consternation I saw that all the onlookers standing round the edge of the floor were laughing too. In spite of myself I felt a spurt of somewhat hysterical laughter well up inside me at my partner's antics, and next time I met Vi's eyes I could not control it and was soon laughing as much as everyone else. At last the music stopped and I made my way back to Vi who immediately grabbed my arm and hustled me to the ladies' cloakroom.

"What on earth possessed you to get on the floor with him?" she demanded.

"Oh, he snook up behind me and I was taken unawares" I said.

"You should've left him in the middle of the floor" said Vi. "He just made a show of you doing a rain dance round you that way."

"Oh, well, I didn't like to do that Vi" I said "he hardly speaks a word of English and it must be lonely wandering round by yourself not knowing anyone."

"Lonely" snorted Vi "not him! Not with the gall he has!" She started to laugh again. "Oh, if you could only have seen your face! Long as a wet week it was! Even the band were laughing, do you know that? That chap playing the trumpet just had to give up. He couldn't blow a note and had to go and try and hide himself behind the big drum. It just isn't safe to let you out on your own, now is it Jen?" she said affectionately.

Hammersmith Palais was always the favourite place to go dancing for Vi and I. There were usually two bands playing during the evening, a resident one and a visiting one, usually a well-known special attraction. The place would be crammed with servicemen of all nationalities and pretty girls in pretty dresses, all amazingly well dressed in view of the stringent clothes rationing during the war years.

It was a warm summer evening, the war in Europe was over at last, and the huge ballroom was literally humming as Vi and I made our way in. Vi was a slim brown-eyed redhead, not really pretty, but vivacious and fun loving. She was popular and once she made contact with someone she liked she was usually gone for the evening. I envied Vi her gaiety and zest for enjoyment and wished I could be more like her.

"You take everything too seriously Jen" she said to me on many occasions. "Remember we are all just ships passing in the night, so relax and have a good time."

The evening was well advanced when Vi rejoined me with a tall, fair haired young GI in tow.

"Come on, Jen" she said "we'll all go and have a cool drink. This is Brad."

"Hi, Jenny" said Brad as he put a hand under the elbow of each of us and steered us to the stairs leading to the balcony, where we sat down at a table overlooking the dance floor while Brad went in search of the drinks. He returned in a short while and deposited several bottles of minerals and straws on the table and excused himself saying he would get his buddy and be back in a few minutes. He soon reappeared with his friend whom he introduced as Gib. Gib was twenty-two, he was tall, he was dark, and he was very good-looking. He was also very quiet and reserved, nothing like the popular image of the brash young GI and nothing like the exuberant Brad. In fact their personalities were so unalike that I wondered what could have drawn them together as friends, because friends they undoubtedly were. As the evening progressed it became apparent that they had a great regard for one another.

Vi and Brad, of course, almost monopolised the conversation, Vi teasing, Brad wisecracking, until the band struck up a very popular tune of the moment, when they jumped up and sped down the stairs and on to the floor leaving

Gib and I rather floundering round trying to make conversation. Gib apologised for not asking me to dance explaining that he was a poor dancer, but that when something slower was played perhaps I would risk a turn or two with him. I nodded and turned my attention to the floor where several couples had started jitterbugging to the racy music, and I loved to watch. There were always a few couples who were really expert, and gradually the crowd left the floor gathering round to watch in delight and at the end of the display raise an appreciative cheer for the hot, dishevelled, breathless couples.

When the dance ended, the two boys walked us to the Tube station to catch our train home before getting a taxi for themselves as they were going in the opposite direction and were unfamiliar with London. We settled down for the ride and Vi was full of Brad. She had enjoyed the evening enormously! "And how did you get on with Gib, Jen?" she asked at length.

"Oh, he's nice enough, Vi" I replied "but we could hardly find a word to say to one another apart from that famous phrase 'Do you come here often?' that is" and we both giggled.

"Well it couldn't have been that bad" said Vi "because while you were getting your coat we arranged to make up a foursome for tomorrow evening, and I can tell you he was quite pleased at the idea."

"Oh, no, Vi" I said.

"Oh, yes!" said Vi definitely. "It's all arranged! We're going to the fair in Abbotts Park and afterwards back home for a sandwich. So you will come, won't you, Jen?" she said coaxingly.

"Oh, I don't know Vi" I said dubiously.

"Well, now, I'll tell you about Gib" said Vi "Brad told me all about him" and she proceeded to tell me that Brad and Gib had met in a prisoner of war camp. They were not in the same unit and Gib had been captured some time before Brad. He had joined up straight from college and been in some fierce fighting before his capture. The food in the camp was very scarce and poor in quality with the result that they were in a very bad state indeed when they were eventually released. They had only just been released from a rehabilitation centre, and both were awaiting passage home.

"So you see, Jen" continued Vi "you can hardly expect him to be a laugh-a-minute yet can you?"

"No" I said "you can't!"

"So you will come then" said Vi "because Brad wants to keep a bit of an eye on him for a while."

"Oh, all right then" I said "it's a date!"

The next evening, therefore, we all met as arranged and had an enjoyable evening sampling the hobby-horses, helter-skelter and chair o'planes, which was all the small fair had to offer; and though Gib still did not have a lot to say he seemed happy enough as he caught hold of my hand and smiled down at me gravely.

In the weeks that followed Gib and I spent many happy hours wandering round London. Gib was from British stock and wanted to see as much as possible in order "to tell the folks back home" all about it as he said. He took particular interest in "Speaker's Corner" in Hyde Park professing amazement at some of the views expressed saying he did not know of anything like it back home and that some of those guys would be in danger of being lynched if they said such things in his home town. He was also very interested in the speakers from the various religions and though he confessed to having no commitment to any particular faith he often made the remark "There sure weren't any atheists in our foxholes!"

During this time Gib was rather short of money, to his way of thinking anyway, as he said his records had to be sorted out and he was only given a token payment on account each day. Privately I thought he was still rather affluent, and, anyway, I preferred the smaller cafes and the cheaper seats at the shows and pictures, as I was used to.

One evening as we were wandering round we came to one of the poshest hotels in London and lingered outside listening to the strains of music wafting through the doors.

"Some sort of a tea dance going on in there" said Gib. "Let's go in."

"Oh we can't go in there" I said "it costs about six bob to look at a sandwich in there, let alone eat one."

Gib laughed but promised me that when he got paid in full we would most certainly go.

Soon after this on a fine Sunday afternoon I set out as usual to meet Gib. The arranged meeting place was Piccadilly Circus. Every GI in London knew Piccadilly Circus, and when I emerged from the Tube station it seemed to me that every GI in London was also meeting his girl there that afternoon. I felt rather conspicuous as I waited for Gib, who, unusually for him was late. I shrank back into a doorway hoping that Gib would spot me, in my cheerful check coat, much more easily that I could spot him in that sea of khaki. That check coat was the only good one that I possessed, so, of course, I wore it constantly, and when Gib had casually remarked on that fact one day I launched into an explanation of the strict clothes rationing in force during the war. Gib had been sympathetic saying that pretty girls should have nice things, but I said it was not important, everyone was in the same boat, and the only important thing was that the war was over and that we were all safe.

"When I get back home I'll get Mom to send you something nice" promised Gib.

The time went by slowly and still no Gib, and I began to feel apprehensive. I wondered if he had already embarked for home, and I thought of the many other young men who had come into my life for a short while and then gone out of it without, in many instances, my really knowing what had happened to them. A constantly shifting population continuously on the move which made any enduring friendships rather difficult, and I wondered whether Gib was to be another of those "ships that just passed in the night" and I desperately hoped not.

At last I decided that it was no use waiting any longer and was on the point of turning into the Tube station for my journey home when I heard a shout "Jenny, Jenny" and turned to see Gib hurrying towards me. I ran to meet him, straight into his arms. "Gee, honey" he said, "I didn't think I was going to make it. We've got our passage home and will be off in a few days. We must talk about us and our future. We have a future together, Jen, haven't we?" he asked as he looked down at me anxiously. I nodded happily.

"First of all though I want to keep that promise I made you" he said.

"What was that?" I asked.

"Well we'll go and sample some of those six bob sandwiches you told me of, Jen, just for a start, 'cos I've been paid at last, and tonight this lil'ole town belongs to us."

The Parting of the Ways

Gib set sail for home within a few days but before doing so he bought me a lovely three-diamond twist engagement ring, the most precious and loveliest thing I ever had in my life. Brad, of course, had gone too but Vi was not broken-hearted, although she missed him a lot, and things were flat with her for a while, and she would tell me rather waspishly to stop looking so smug and spend less time "flaunting " my third finger, which I must confess I was guilty of.

Then one day she burst into our office in great excitement.

"You'll never guess what" she said.

"What?" I asked.

"There's four simply gorgeous Australian airmen been assigned to this office for training."

"Really" I said.

"Yes, really" she mimicked. "Simply gorgeous they are. Complete knock-outs in that super navy blue uniform of theirs¡"

Vi's mood changed suddenly and she said to me. "You remember Paddy Finucane, Jen?" she asked.

"Yes, Vi, I remember him!" I said.

The two of us sat thinking our own thoughts. Paddy Finucane had been an Australian airman. One of those dashing, glamorous, Battle of Britain Pilots. Vi and I had followed his career avidly; the aircraft he shot down; his decorations; his engagement. Somehow he was a symbol of

113

hope in those dark days, and we were quite devastated when he was killed.

We did not have time to say more as at that very moment the door opened and the chief clerk ushered in the four men to be introduced, and I had to agree with Vi, knock-outs they were, each and every one. They wore the same uniform as our air force, but in navy blue.

The four were railwaymen in "Civvy Street" and whilst they were awaiting passage home it had been decided to fill the time by giving them some experience and a refresher course. Soon it became a regular practice, when they were on the day shift, to join us in the staff room for coffee and tea, and they came bearing gifts, fruit cake, sweet biscuits, tea, coffee and sugar, most of all sugar, and our little breaks took on a party atmosphere.

Vi, of course, being the only "unspoken for" one amongst us, lapped up all the attention. Hetty had married her childhood sweetheart, the only one she had ever had, the only one she ever wanted, some little time before. Her Bill was still somewhere out in the desert where he had served in the North African Campaign. Vi and I had attended her wedding and small reception where absolute marvels had been performed as regards the cake and other refreshments with everyone chipping in with a little bit here and a little bit there out of our meagre rations. One guest proudly proffered a plate of cup cakes in which she told us she had used liquid paraffin as a substitute for the precious and scarce butter and margarine. They certainly looked OK but neither Vi nor I could be prevailed upon to try one. After all, as Vi said laughingly to me "You couldn't be sure what the "end" result would be, could you?"

Hetty was always very kind to us two "Flibberty-gibbets", always interested and amused by our doings. She gave me a very attractive bracelet as a remembrance of her. I have it still and would never part with it as Hetty very tragically lost her life in that horrendous Harrow and Wealdstone train crash some years later.

"Which one of the boys do you think is the nicest?" Vi asked me one day.

"I think Tim is" I replied.

Tim was not particularly good-looking but he had a nice pleasant face. His hair had a decided russet tint, and his skin also, tanned with the healthy red showing through. He smoked a pipe and would puff contentedly during all the banter.

"Oh, I thought you'd say that" said Vi. "I've noticed the way he follows you out whenever you go to make the tea, and how he makes a point of bringing you the best part of his food parcels from home."

"What he brings is shared amongst us as you very well know Vi" I said indignantly.

"Well just don't forget you're spoken for" said Vi.

"I won't forget indeed, Vi" I said huffily.

Those words "Don't forget you're spoken for" were fast becoming Vi's favourite phrase, and I began to wonder if she had a greater interest in Tim than she was letting on.

As the days passed, I became sure of it, and I also had a sneaking suspicion that Tim was rather taken with Vi if the expression in his brown eyes was anything to go by on a few occasions when I caught him looking at her unawares. So I hatched little schemes to get them together and leave them alone whenever I could and my little game bore fruit, literally, as one day Tim presented the three of us, Hetty, Vi and I with a bag of dried fruit each, which he had sent home for specially, as one of us had mentioned that we had forgotten what a real fruity Christmas pudding tasted like. The war was over but luxuries, such as fruit, were in very short supply, indeed rationing continued for quite a long time after the war.

The fruit was very welcome indeed, so much so, that my mother and Vi's mother both said that we must do something to return the thoughtfulness and kindness of that young man, and so we arranged that we would ask him to share a Sunday with us, lunch at Vi's and tea with my family.

Vi was uncharacteristically nervous about broaching the subject with Tim, and rather dithered about it, but as the main invitation was to her home, she had to do it.

"How shall I go about it, Jen?" she asked. "I don't like making the first approach like this. I don't want him to think me forward and trying to worm my way in."

"Well, you are, Vi, aren't you?" I said amidst her hot

denials. "Now don't say that you're not interested in him because I know you too well by this time not to know that you are!"

"He is nice, I must admit" said Vi "but what shall I say to him?"

"Why not just say the truth, that he has been very generous to us and that both our families would like to meet him?"

So the invitation was issued and accepted with alacrity on the part of Tim. I was invited to lunch also so there were six of us; Vi's parents, Vi, Tim and myself and Vi's brother, Dave. Dave had not long come home after having spent five long, long years in a German prisoner-of-war camp. The thing he seemed to resent most was that one of the guards had taken his false teeth for some reason, there were no gold teeth, as I asked that question, so I wondered just why. Anyway, Dave was very annoyed at having to get another set of teeth fitted and fretted at the rather lengthy time it was taking. He was also rather moody and restless, which was a cause of great anxiety to his parents as they watched the first great joy and thankfulness just to be back home evaporate, and this sense of being unable to settle down to the small family electrical repair business again took its place. I, of course, had not known Dave before he went away, but I tried to imagine what I would feel like if I had lost five whole years — years just marking time — out of my life, and I could well understand Dave's sense of disorientation from his family and friends. He just needed time to adapt and to find his niche again.

Vi was anxious also as to how Dave would react to Tim as there had always been a sense of jealousy between the boys in khaki and the more glamorous boys in airforce blue, or as they contemptuously called them "the Brylcreem boys", and there was no doubt that the poor old infantry had got a very sticky end of the stick as usual. However, she need not have worried as everything went off very well, as the three men swapped stories. Vi's father, like my own, had served in the First World War, and the same thing happened when we spent the evening at my home, with Jack gazing goggle-eyed and open-mouthed at each of them as the yarns unfolded.

Jack missed everything by a matter of a few weeks, but he did get into uniform later doing his National Service, spending some time in Egypt, and eventually emigrating to New Zealand.

Tim soon became a regular visitor to our homes, and a very welcome one, and when Vi announced her, to me anyway, expected engagement, we were all very happy for her; though both sets of parents definitely did not like the idea that we would both be going so far from them.

One evening Vi's mother seemed very interested in a certain place in Australia and plied Tim with questions about it to such an extent that we all became curious, and on the next occasion, when the three of us were together and enjoying a cup of tea, Vi tackled her as to the reason for her questions. She left the room and when she returned she had a bundle of letters in her hand, selected one, and handed it to us in turn to read. It was written in the most beautiful copperplate script; a sad letter, a letter from a rejected suitor and bearing an address in the area in which she had shown such interest. It read : —

My dear Bea,

I received your letter this morning. I cannot say I was glad to get it. It was a real body-blow to me and has destroyed all my hopes for the future. I have been working extremely hard to gather enough together to enable me to take a holiday with you and have something to make a home for the two of us here.

I realise that your father only had your best interests at heart, and I respect him for that, but it has made things very hard for me. If he had only allowed you to come out here to me I could have sent your fare, and my parents were looking forward to welcoming you into the family.

However there's no point in going into that now and it only remains for me to wish you every happiness in the future, and that is a very sincere wish, as I think you will surely know. However, if anything does go wrong with your present plans, please do not hesitate to write to me at once.

Devotedly yours,
Pete

"Well, you're a deep one" said Vi "you never said a word about this all these years."

"Well, what was the point" said her mother.

"What does that bit about your father having your best interests at heart mean?" asked Vi.

Her mother then told her that she had met this Australian soldier towards the end of the First World War. She had been a nanny to two children whose parents managed a very well-known London hotel. It was a nice job, but she was very lonely as she had come up from the Midlands, personally known to her employers, of course, and in their charge, but she knew no one of her own age except for the downstairs staff and she was forbidden to go out with them. She used to sneak out with them, however, whenever she got the chance and once when she was caught her mistress gave her a good beating saying she had undertaken to be responsible for her to her parents. On one of these outings she had met Pete and as the friendship progressed he was introduced to her employers and then her parents and family who all approved. They got engaged, but before they could be married, Pete was sent home. Her father had insisted that she could not go all that way unless she was married and escorted by her husband, and she did not dream of disobeying her father in any way. So time passed and then she met Vi's father and married him.

"And you kept the letter all this time?" said Vi.

"Of course I kept the letter. I was very young and impressionable. It is part of my tender and romantic youth" said Vi's mother with a smile.

"What was his surname?" asked Vi. "You never know I might run across him one day."

"Well that I think I'll keep to myself" said her mother. "It's all water under the bridge now. But I thought you might be interested in the coincidence."

So that is how, in the course of time, Vi and I ended up on opposite sides of the world. We were not destined to meet again for thirty years.